The Road Home From Skye

SCOTTISH & IRISH TUNES FOR CELTIC HARP | BY STEPHANIE CLAUSSEN

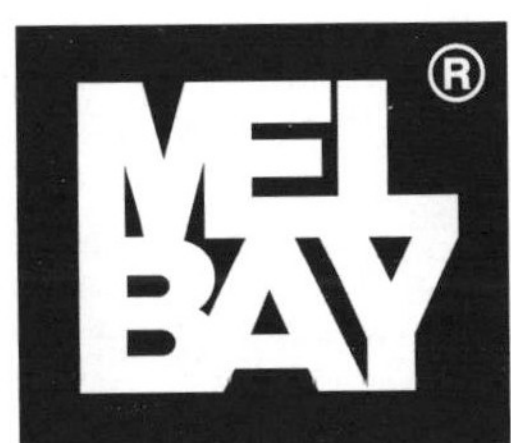

WWW.MELBAY.COM

Notes

When I first started learning the harp, I thought I had to play everything on the page exactly as written. In the decades since then I've learned that the musician actually has a lot of freedom when it comes to interpreting a piece. With that in mind, I encourage you to adjust these arrangements to fit your current playing level and musical taste; simplify, shorten, or adapt at will.

-Stephanie

Consistent bracketing and fingering are both desperately important in order to play this music smoothly and confidently. Write in your fingering; write in your brackets!

Dynamics are what bring the music to life. Include them from the very first play through.

Flat hand: For the most part, all left-hand octaves, 9ths and 10ths (as well as most single notes in the left hand) should be played with a flat hand. This will help you achieve a crisp and clean bass sound that doesn't grow too muddy.

Rests, ties and muffles: I've used rests to indicate when to muffle the left-hand accompaniment in some way (usually by placing the next chord early) and ties to indicate that you should let the notes ring. But you may decide you like to play things differently. I've included actual muffle signs only when I consider a muffle absolutely essential to the arrangement.

Grace notes: Feel free to add more ornaments, skip them entirely, or improvise your own. If you are having trouble with the rhythm of a specific passage, practice it without any ornaments first, then add them back in.

Slurs indicate groups of notes that need to be played as a phrase. This is a *mental* effort as much as it is a physical one! Make sure you can hear the phrase in your head as you play it.

Symbols:

+ Play the note (or octave) with the hand flat against the strings, using either the thumb or fourth finger (or both).

⌖ Muffle

⌒ Cross over or slide

’ Breath mark; come off rather than connect

The tunes in this book can be found on the album *The Road Home From Skye: Scottish and Irish Tunes*. The arrangements have been edited and, in some cases, shortened to better fit the written format.

Contents

Flat Hand Exercises

1. Thumbs and 4th fingers with flat hand position

Place all your fingers flat against the strings, pointing (more or less) upward, with the thumb or 4th finger resting on the note you intend to play. When you place the next note, your flat hand will muffle the previous note; place each note as late as possible to create a smooth, connected sound.

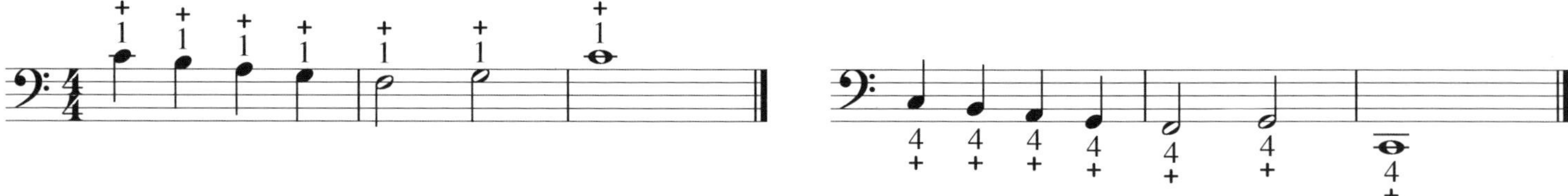

2. Octaves and 10ths with flat hand position

Rest your hand flat against the strings at an angle that allows you to comfortably reach the octave or 10th. Your fingers will probably point away from you with a slight upward angle. Most people use their 4th finger to play the bass note. When you place the next figure, your flat hand will muffle the previous notes; place each interval as late as possible to create a smooth, connected sound.

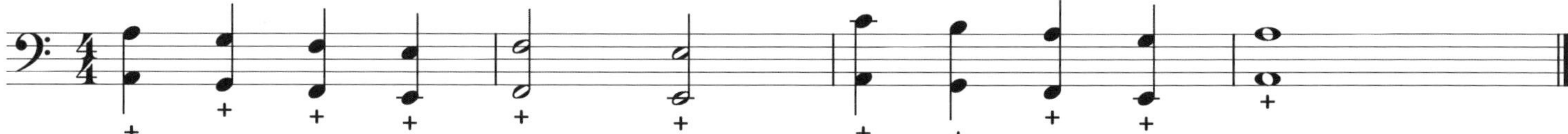

3. Brush Muffles

Any time you play an ascending bass line, you can use a brush muffle to reduce excess ringing in the bass. On your way to placing each ascending octave (with fingers flat against the strings), very gently brush your 4th finger past the bass note of the previous octave so as to muffle it. Brush muffles are not indicated in this book; use your ears to tell you when to use one.

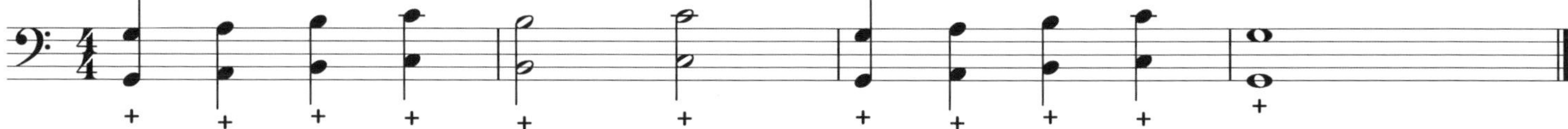

4. Octaves with early placing

To achieve a more rhythmic sound, you can place any figure early, muffling previously ringing strings. Place these octaves very firmly with your fingers completely flat to muffle any ringing strings. In this book, early placing is often indicated by a rest between left hand figures.

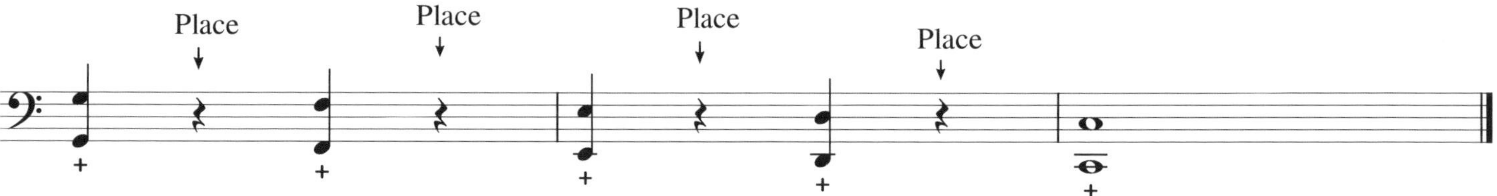

Skye Air

Air, Traditional Scottish
Arranged by Stephanie Claussen

Spacious and lingering

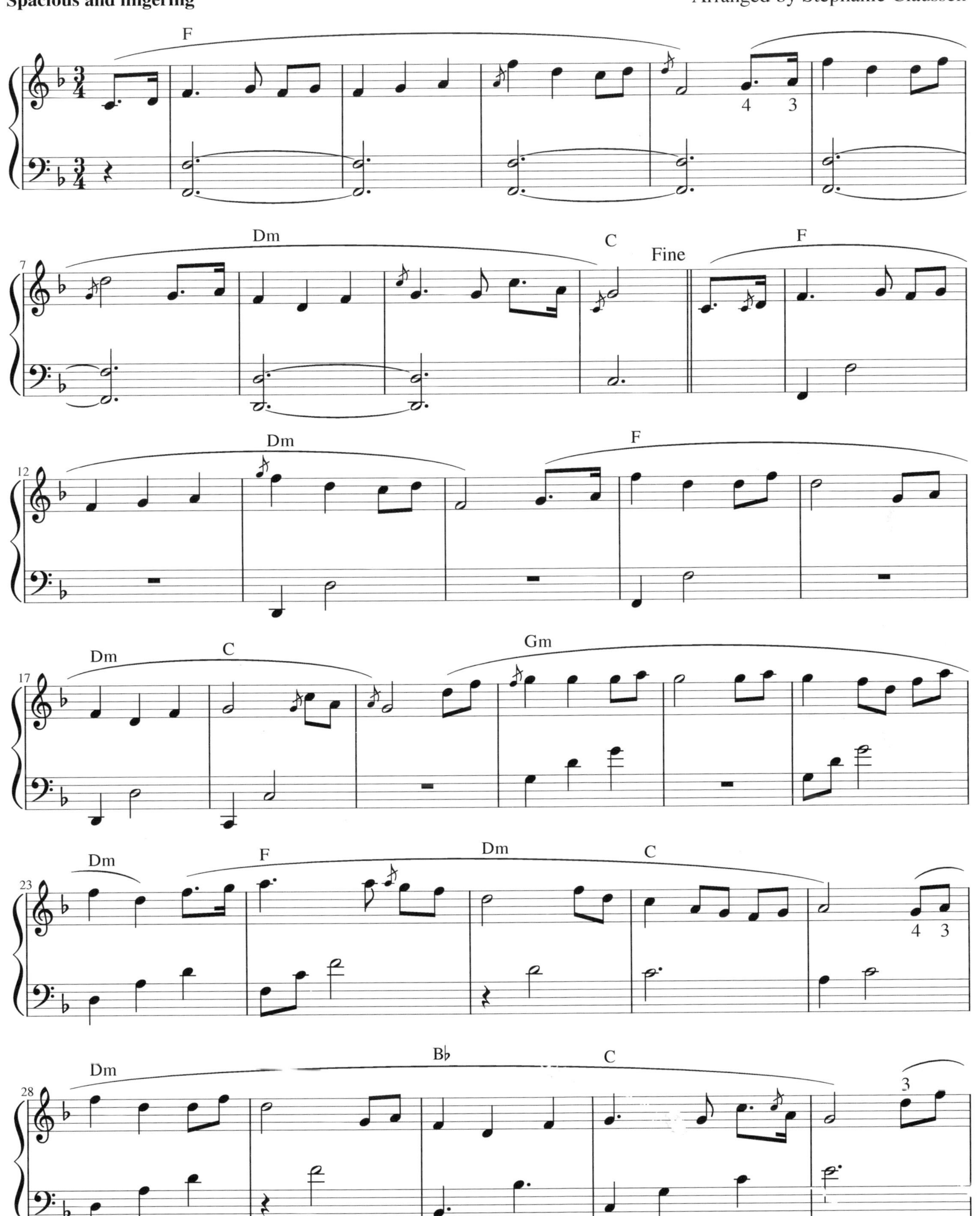

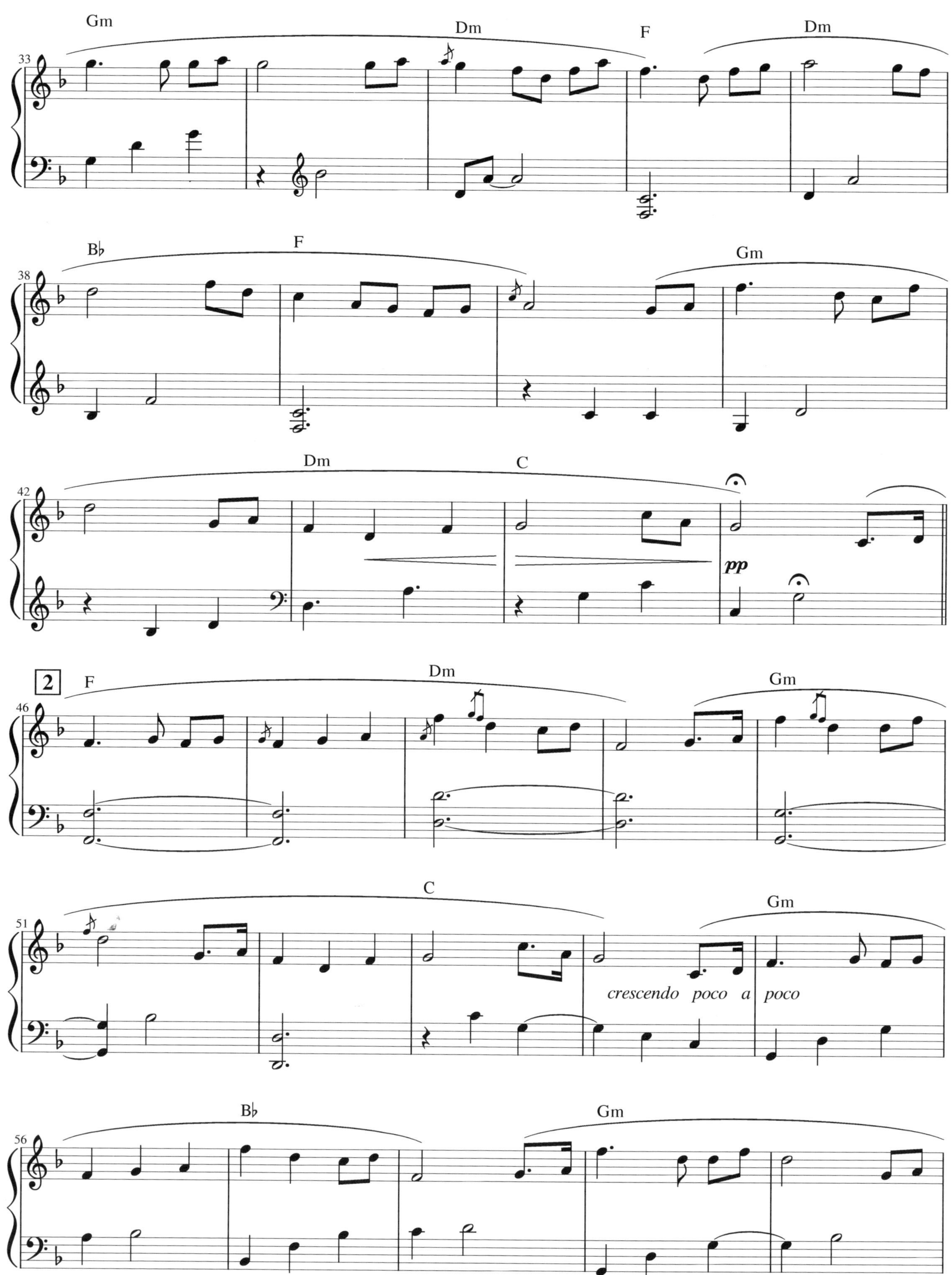
Gm
Dm
F
Dm
B♭
F
Gm
Dm
C
pp
2
F
Dm
Gm
C
Gm
crescendo poco a poco
B♭
Gm

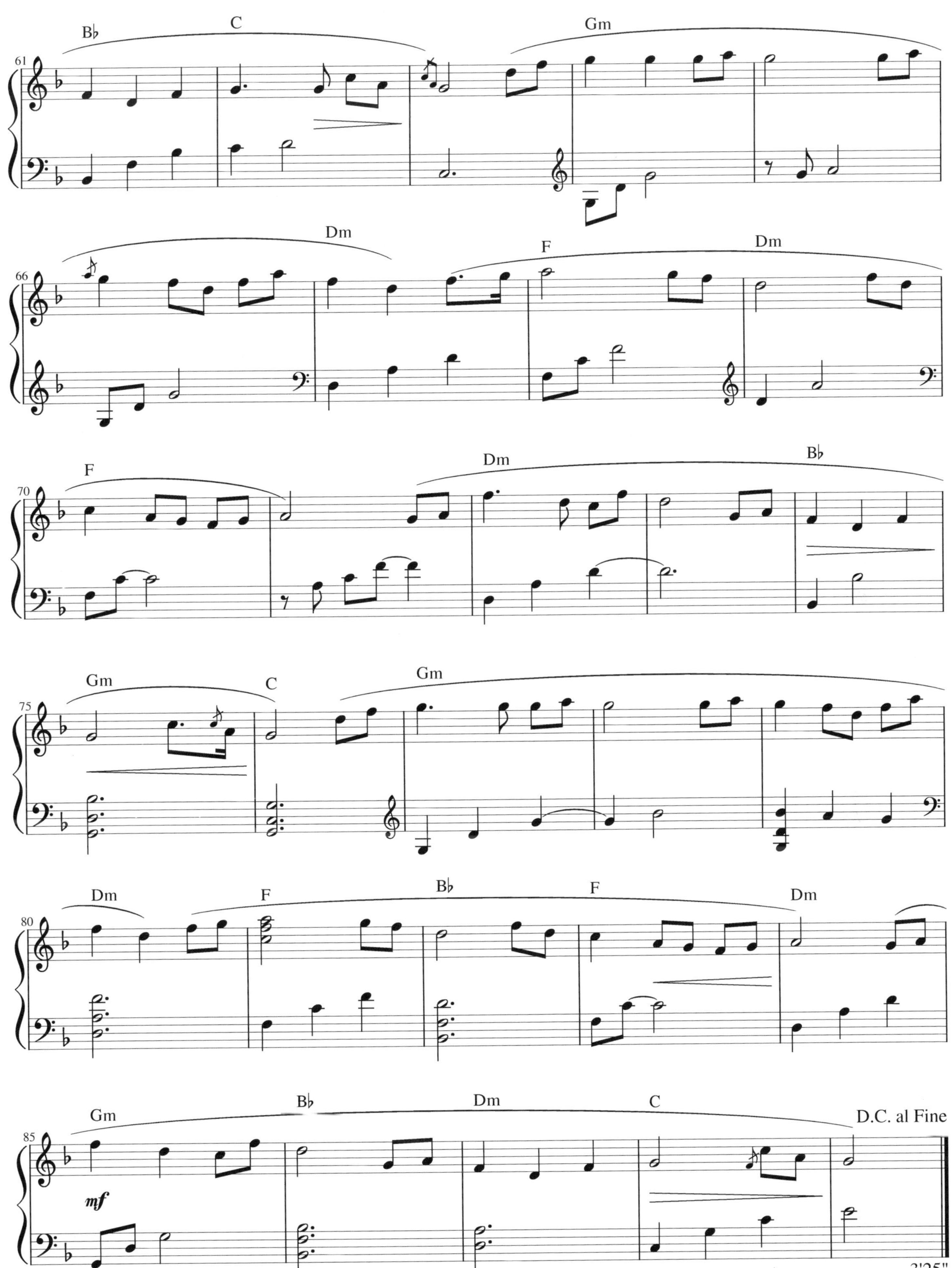
B♭
C
Gm
Dm
F
Dm
F
Dm
B♭
Gm
C
Gm
Dm
F
B♭
F
Dm
Gm
B♭
Dm
C
D.C. al Fine
mf
3'25"

Brose and Butter

Slip jig, Traditional Scottish
Arranged by Stephanie Claussen

Tromping and lazy

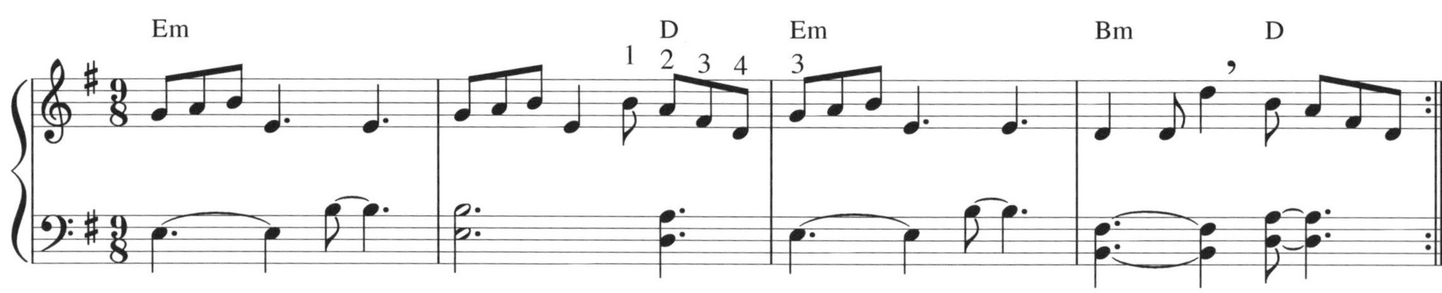

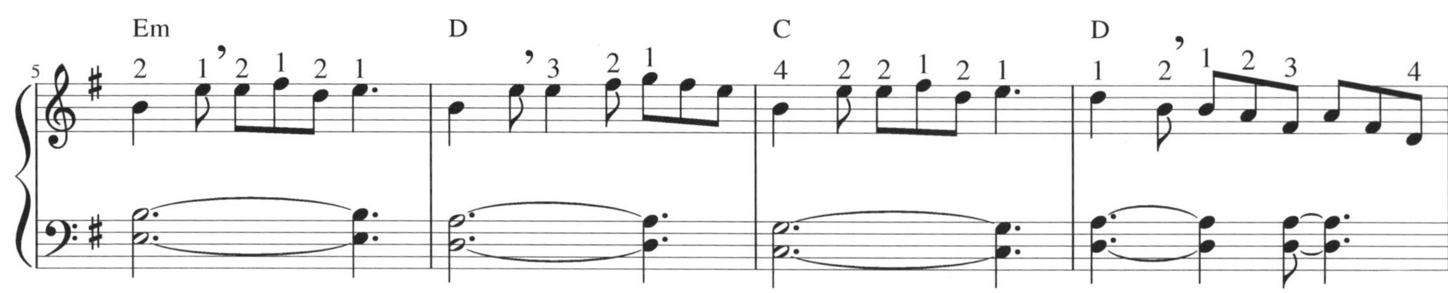

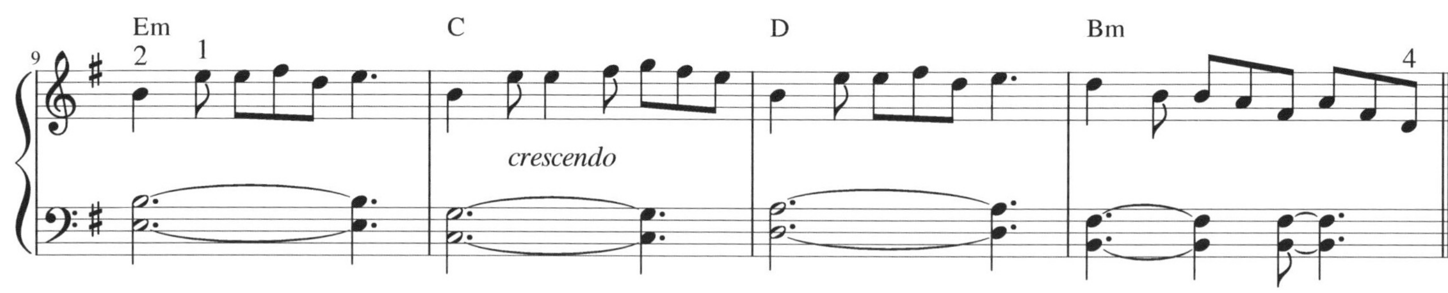

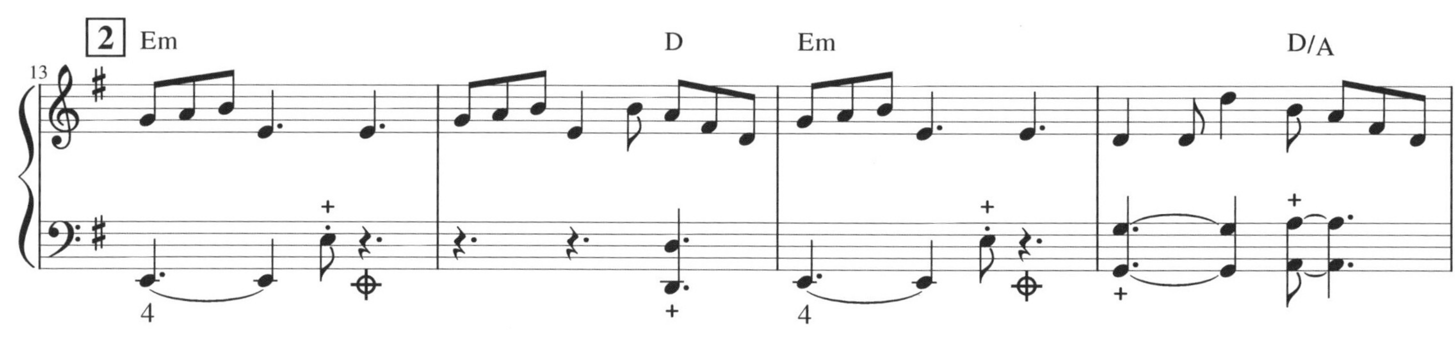

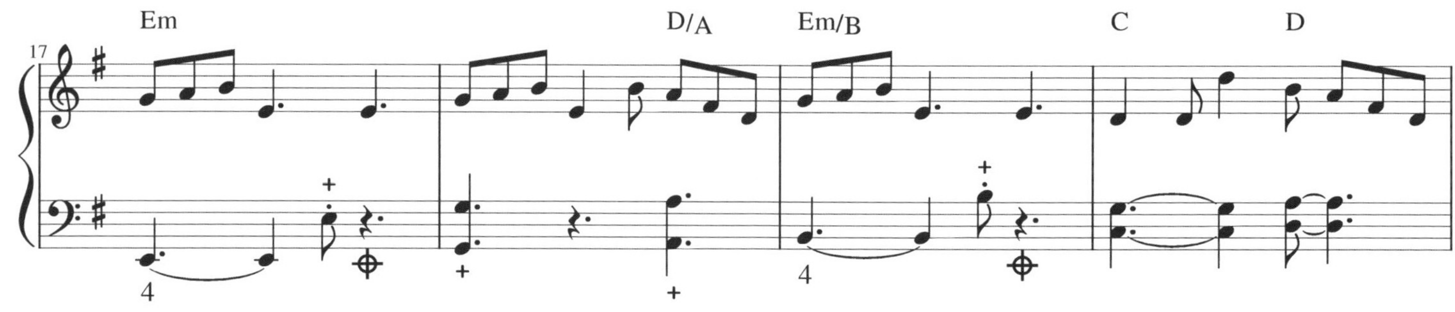

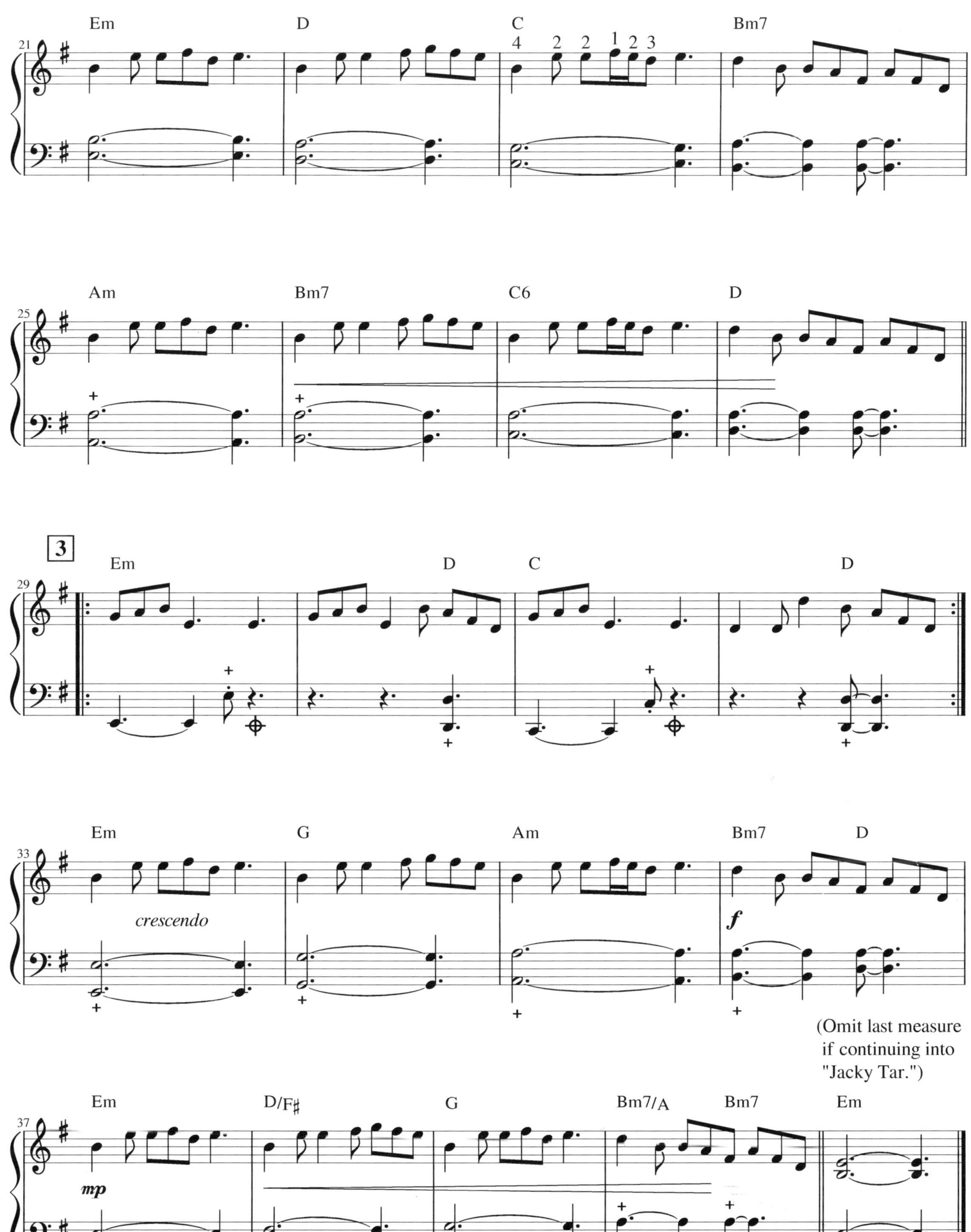
Em
D
C
4 2 2 1 2 3
Bm7
Am
Bm7
C6
D
3
Em
D
C
D
Em
G
Am
Bm7
D
crescendo
f
(Omit last measure
if continuing into
"Jacky Tar.")
Em
D/F♯
G
Bm7/A
Bm7
Em
mp
1'40"

Left-Hand Exercises

1. Switching between regular hand position and flat hand position

Play the arpeggios with your fingers curved downward, and the flat octaves with your fingers flat against the strings pointing upward and away from you. When you place the flat octaves, most of the notes of the previous arpeggio will be muffled.

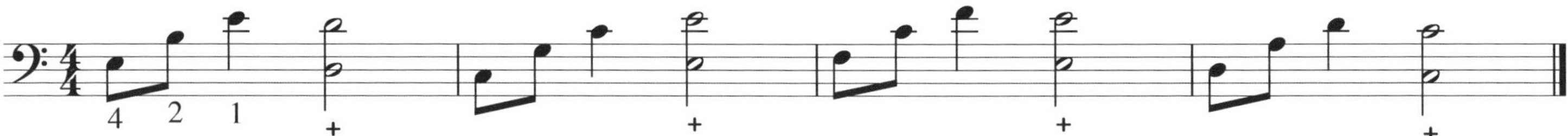

2. Flat hand accompaniment figure

At the beginning of each measure, place the first two notes with your hand flat against the strings. Replace the thumb (still with a flat hand) on beat 3 and play it on beat 4. The bass note will keep ringing through the measure.

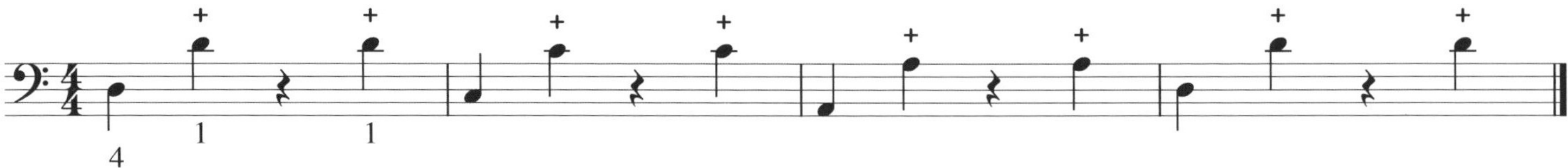

Ornament Exercises

These ornaments require slow practice and lots of repetition before your hand muscles will be "in shape" enough to play them. Relax your hand frequently and listen to yourself; make sure you can hear each note clearly.

1. Two-note ornaments with accent on the first beat

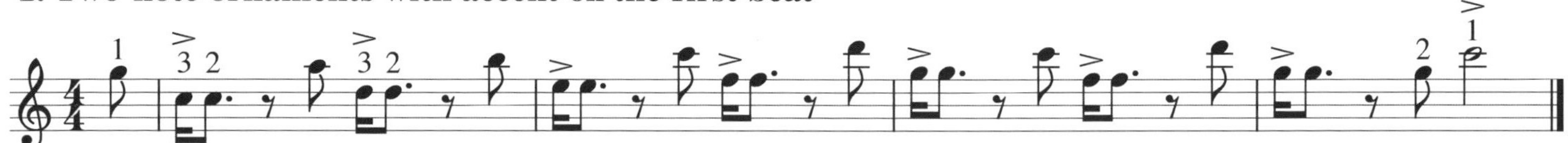

2. Two-note ornaments with accent on the second beat

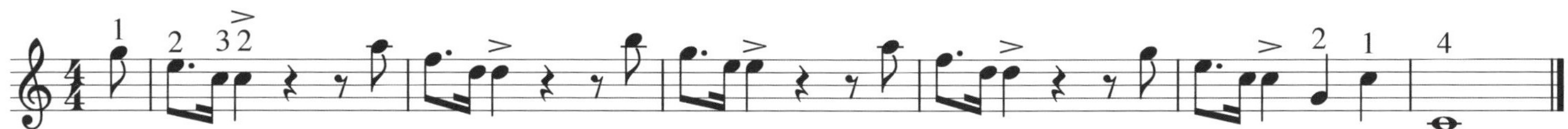

3. Three-note ornaments

Three-note ornaments can be played with a variety of fingerings including 321 and 212. I find that 432 works well for the tunes in this book.

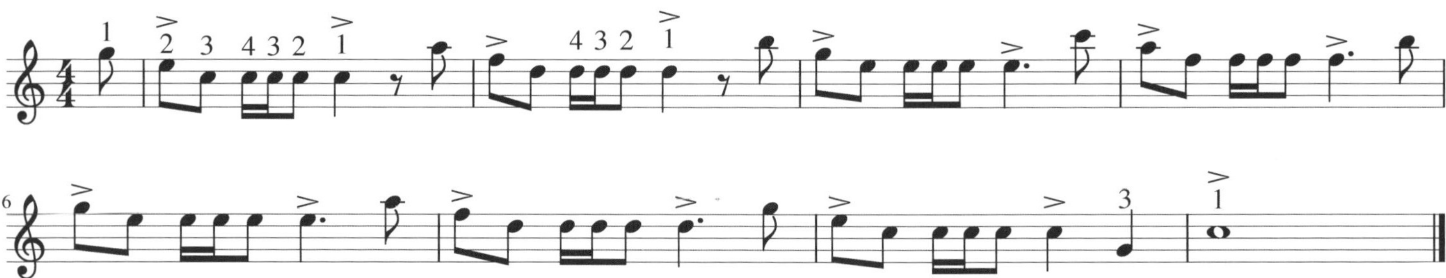

Jacky Tar

Hornpipe, Traditional Scottish
Arranged by Stephanie Claussen

Boisterous and casual

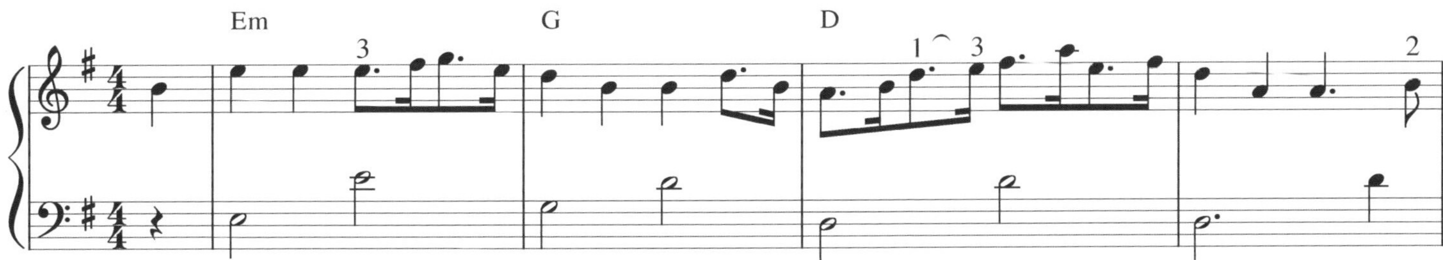

(Omit pickup note if continuing from "Brose and Butter.")

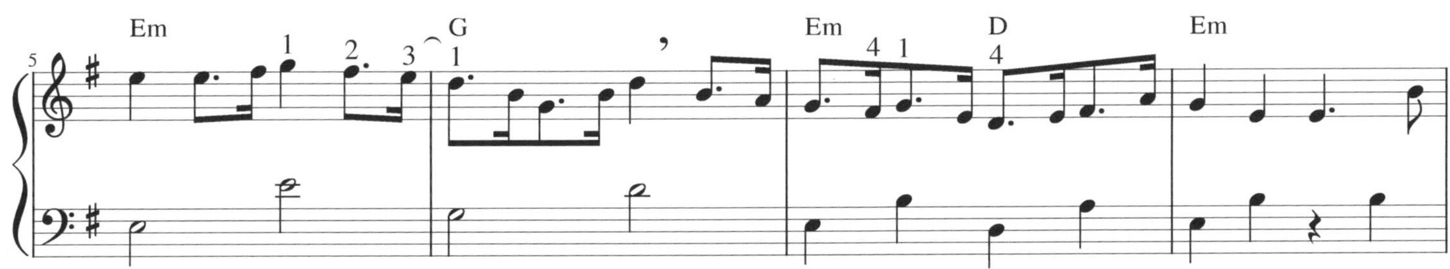

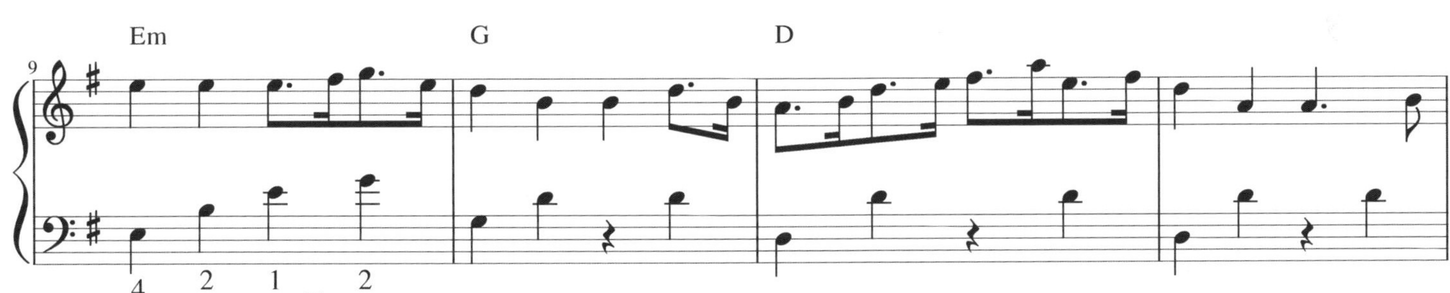

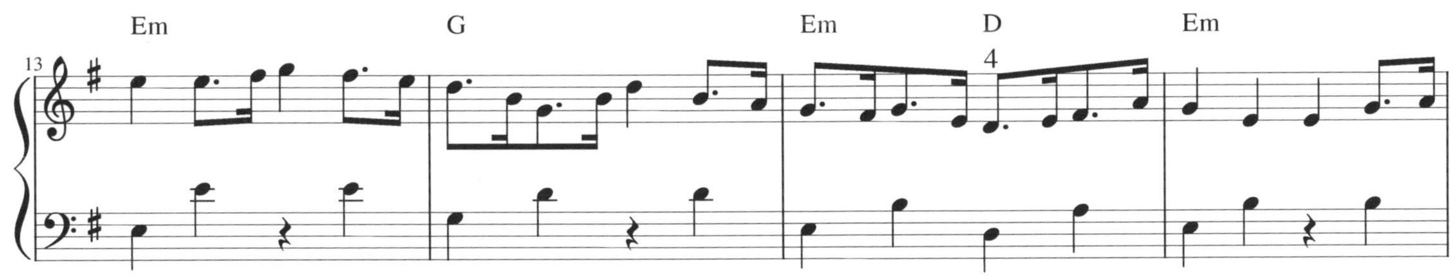

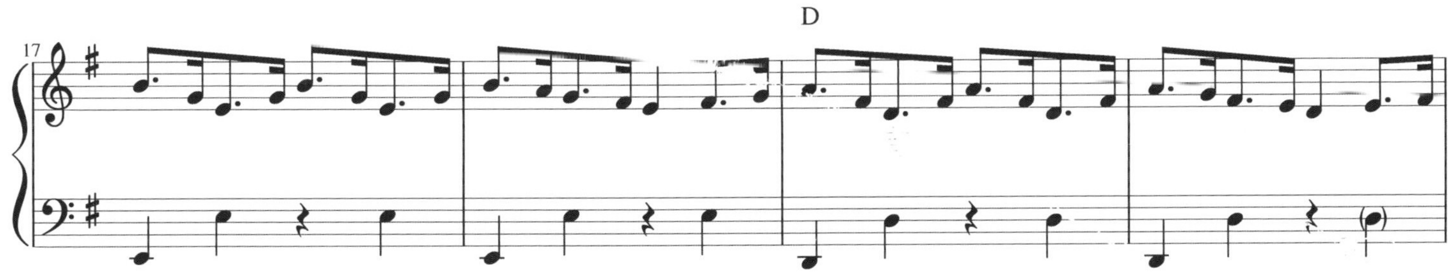

All left-hand octaves, broken or otherwise, should be played flat.

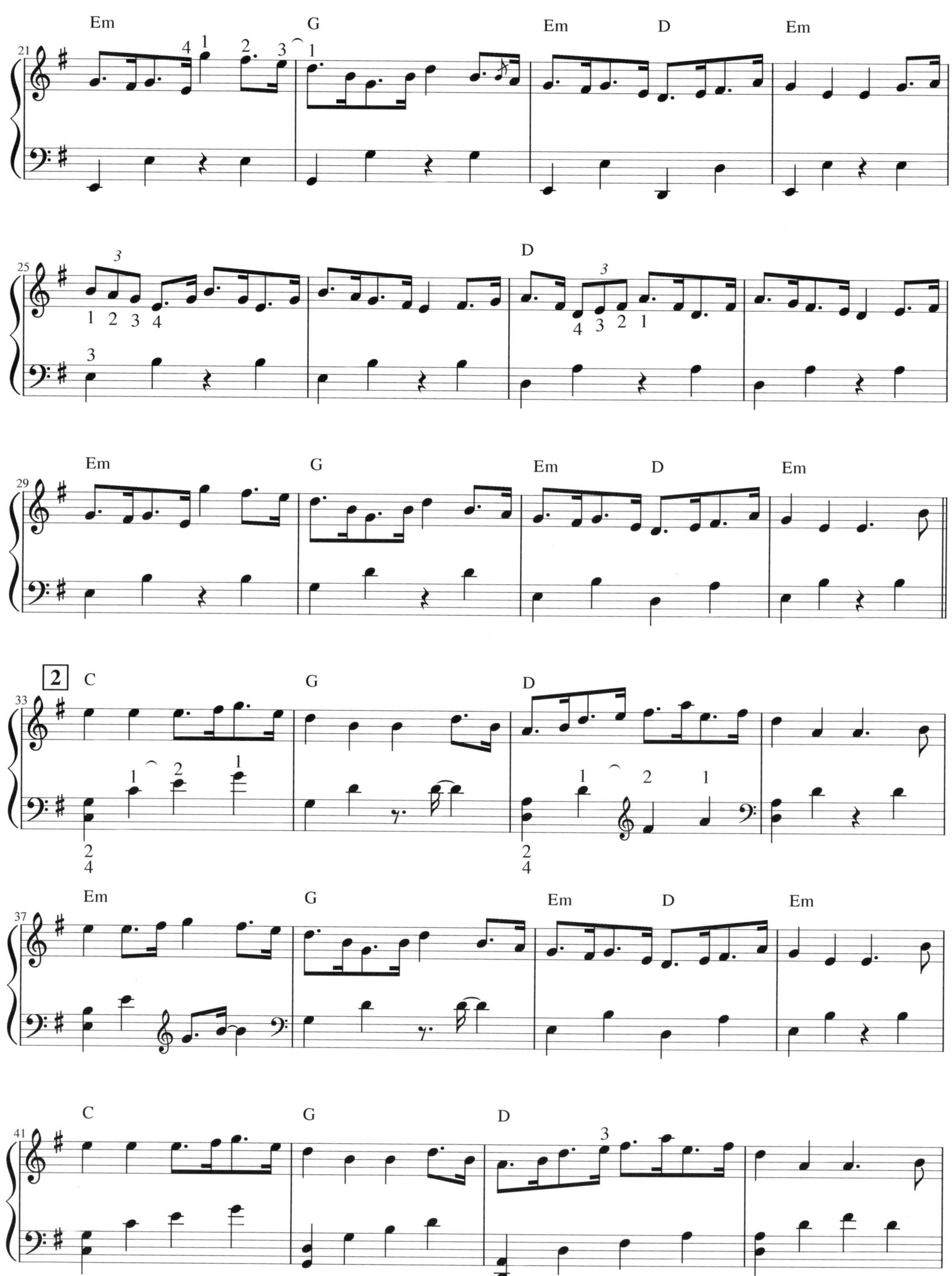
Em
G
Em
D
Em
D
Em
G
Em
D
Em
2
C
G
D
Em
G
Em
D
Em
C
G
D

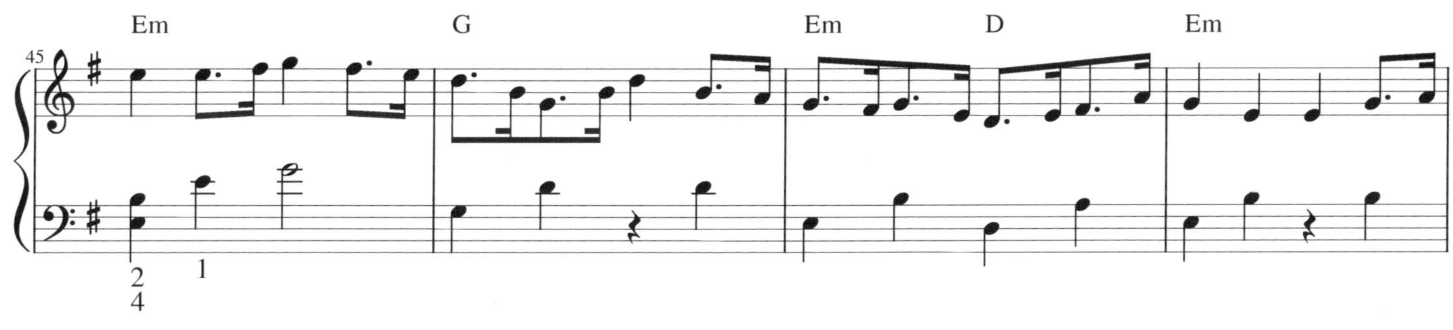

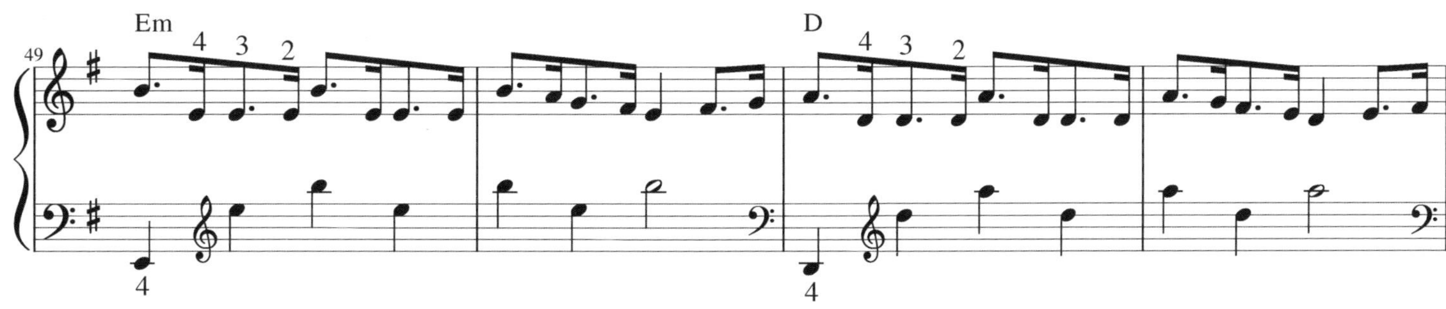

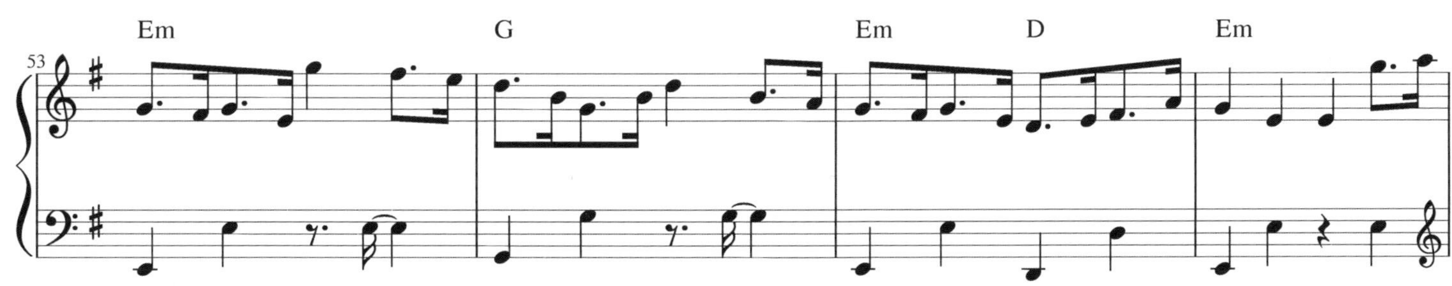

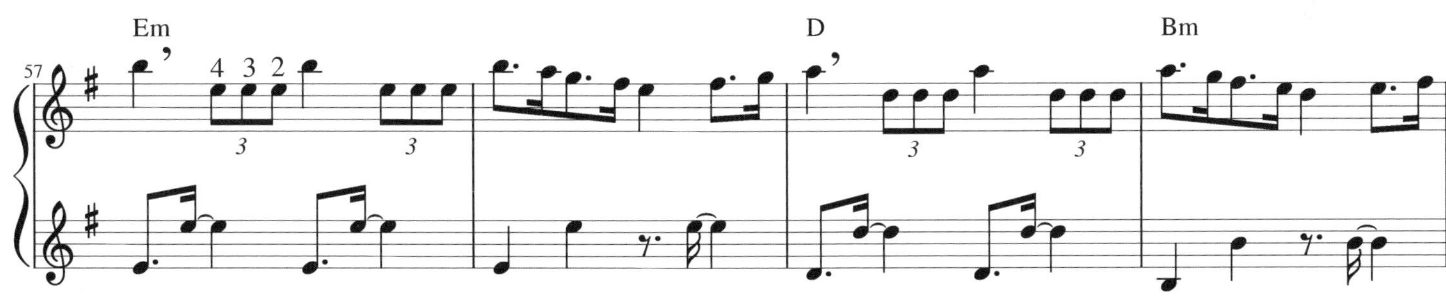

(Alternate last m.
to lead into
"Far From Home")

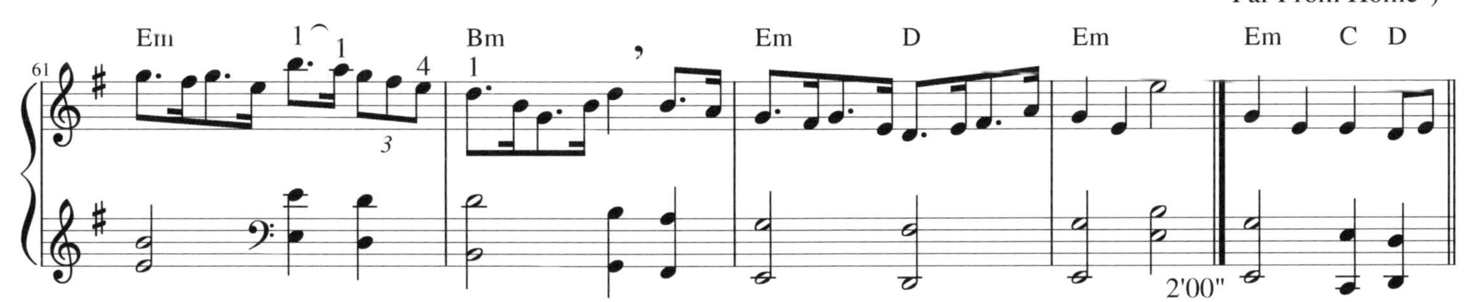

Far From Home

Reel, Traditional
Arranged by Stephanie Claussen

Happily

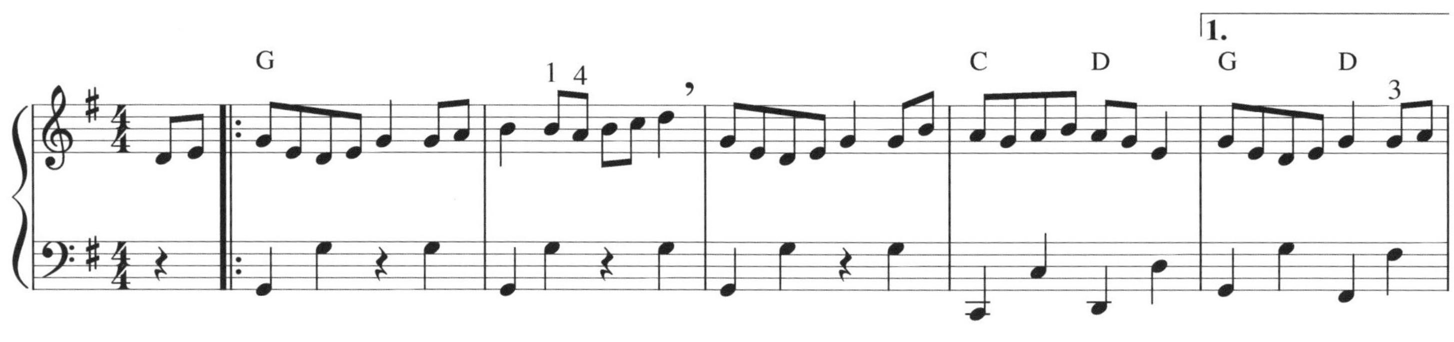

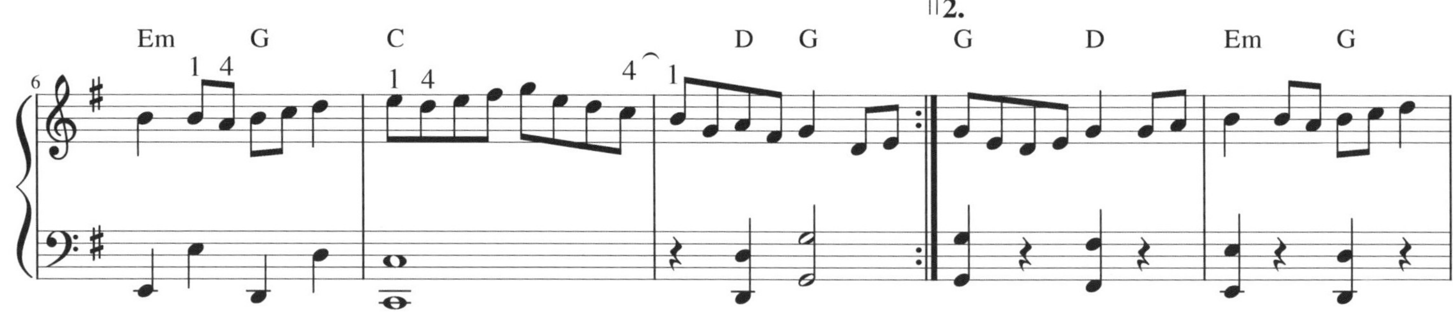

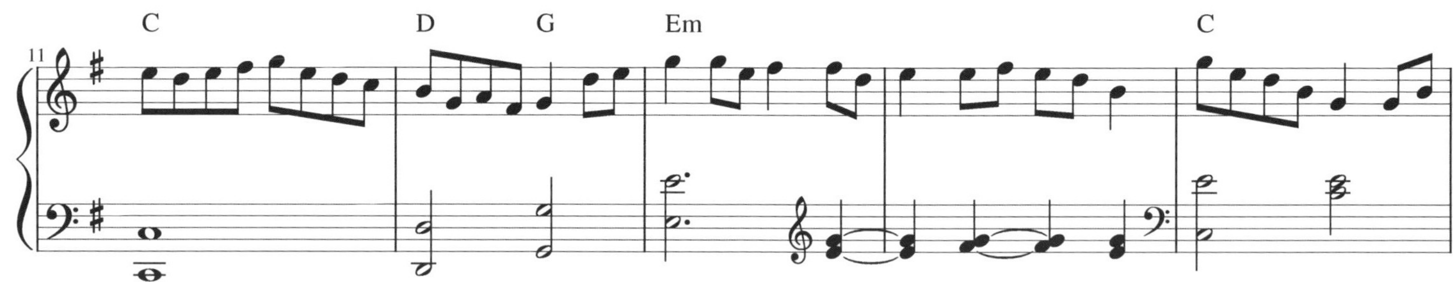

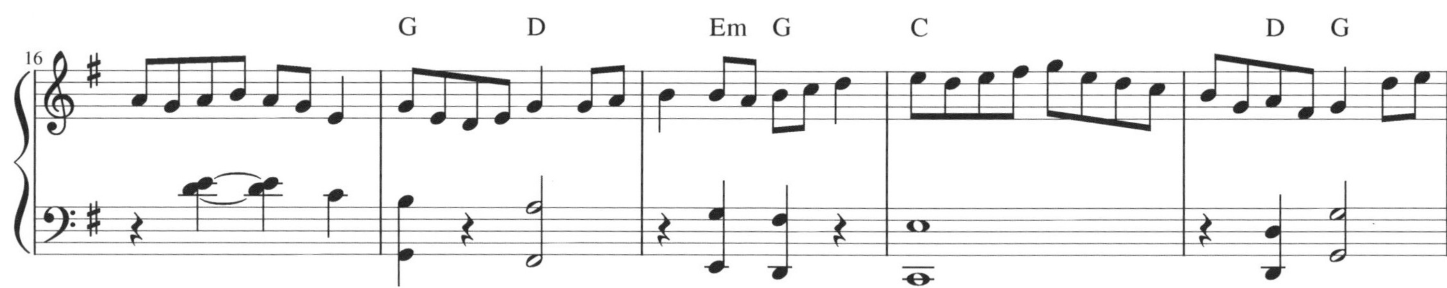

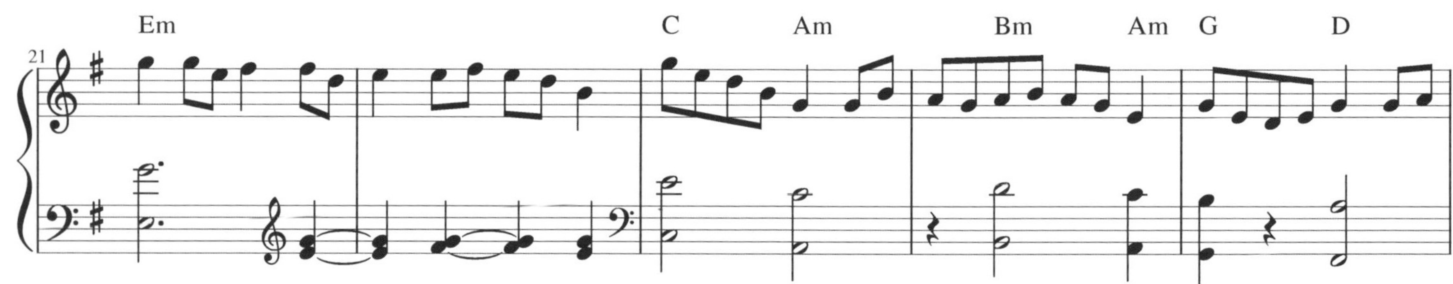

All left-hand octaves and 10ths, broken or otherwise, should be played flat.

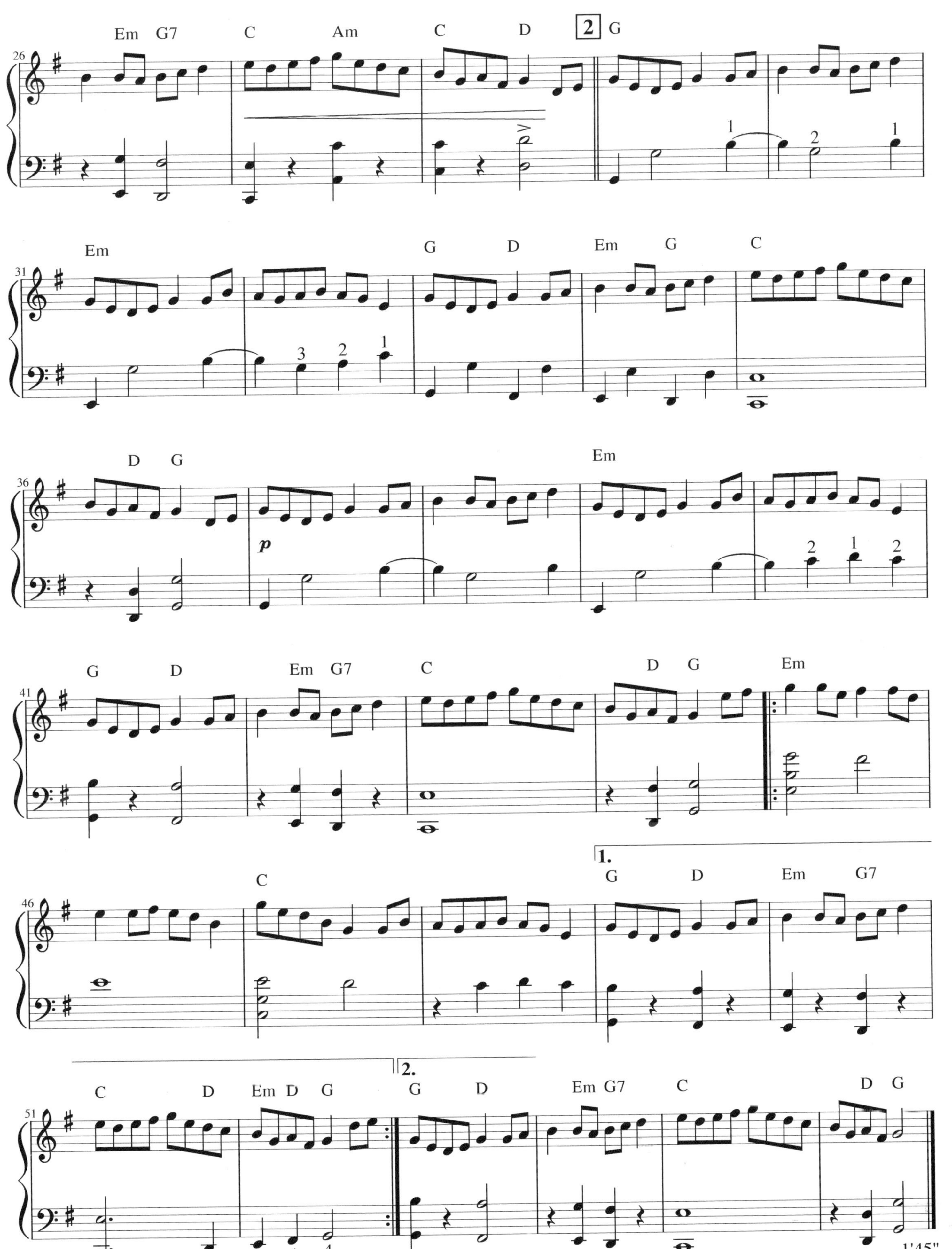
26 Em G7 C Am C D 2 G
31 Em G D Em G C
36 D G Em
p
41 G D Em G7 C D G Em
46 C 1. G D Em G7
51 C D Em D G 2. G D Em G7 C D G
1'45"

Are Ye Sleepin' Maggie?

by Robert Tannahill
Arranged by Stephanie Claussen

Dark and moody

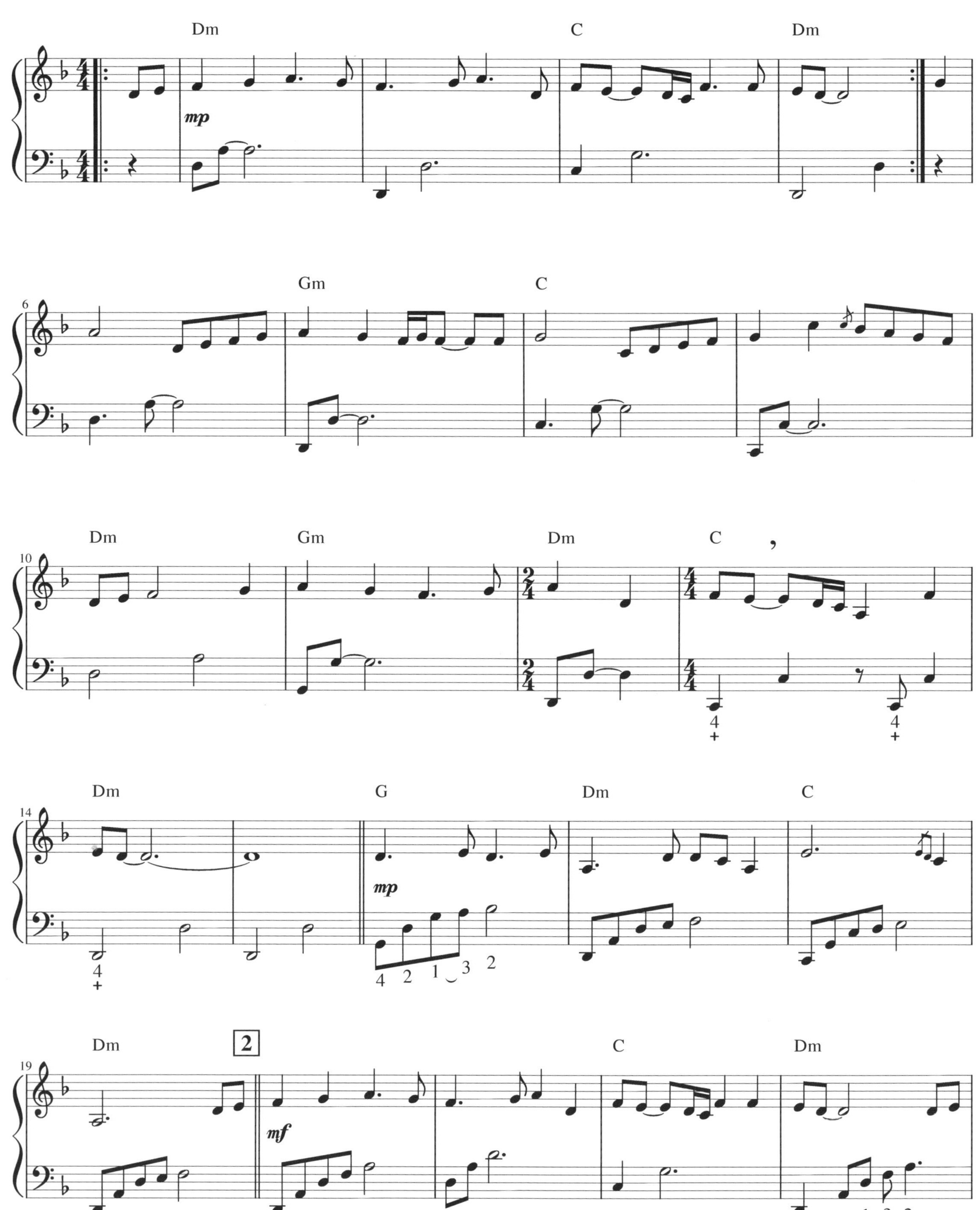

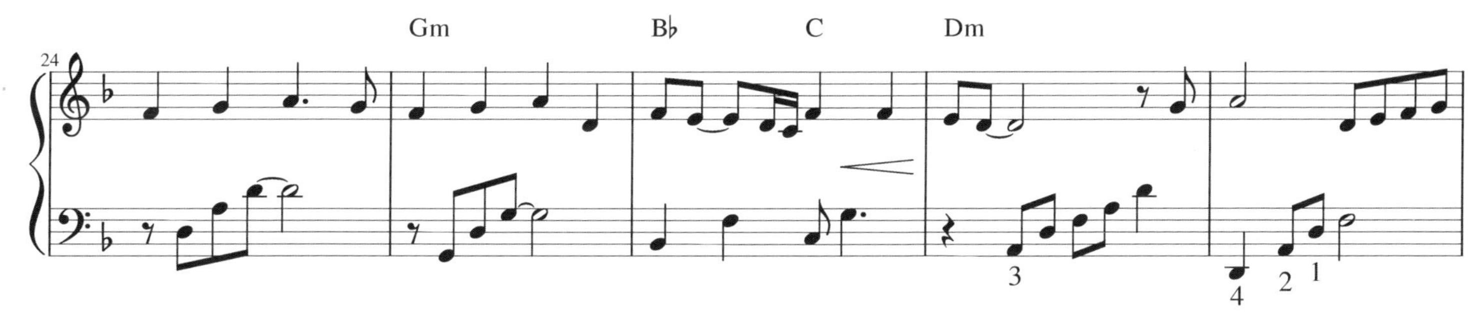
24
Gm
B♭
C
Dm
3
4 2 1

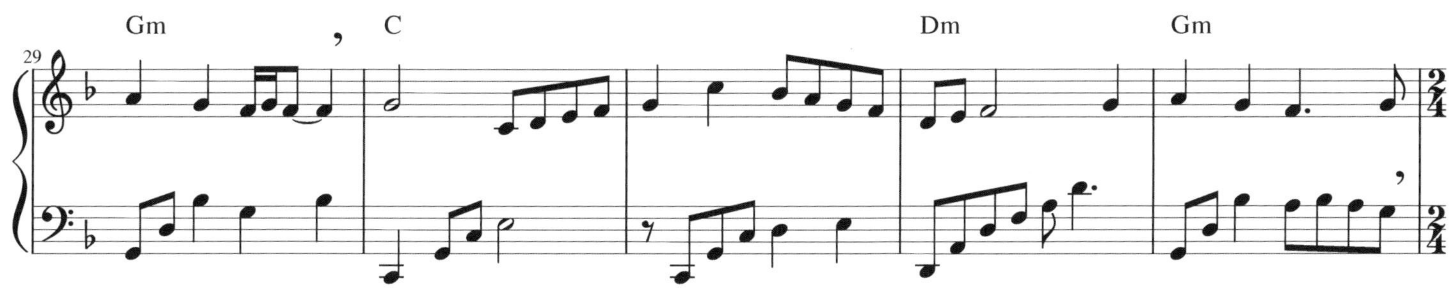
29
Gm
C
Dm
Gm

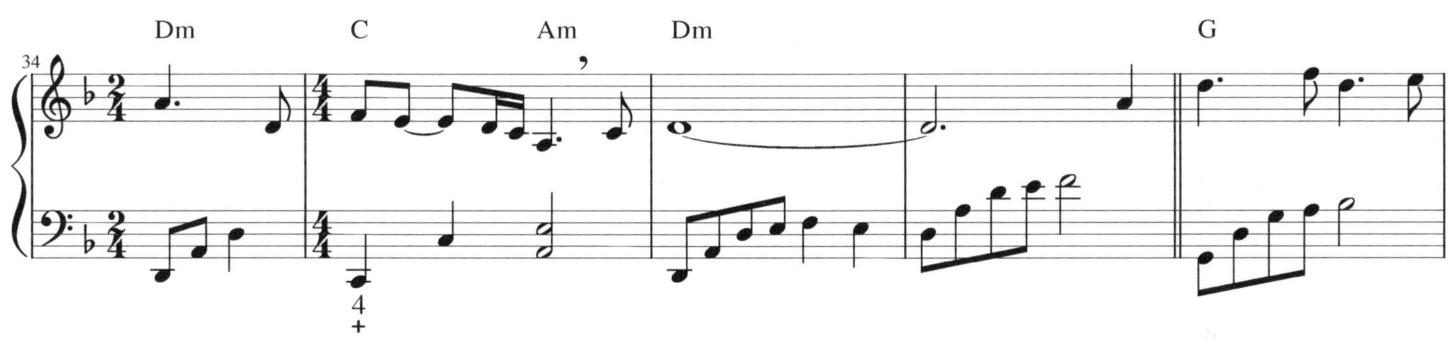
34
Dm
C
Am
Dm
G
4
+

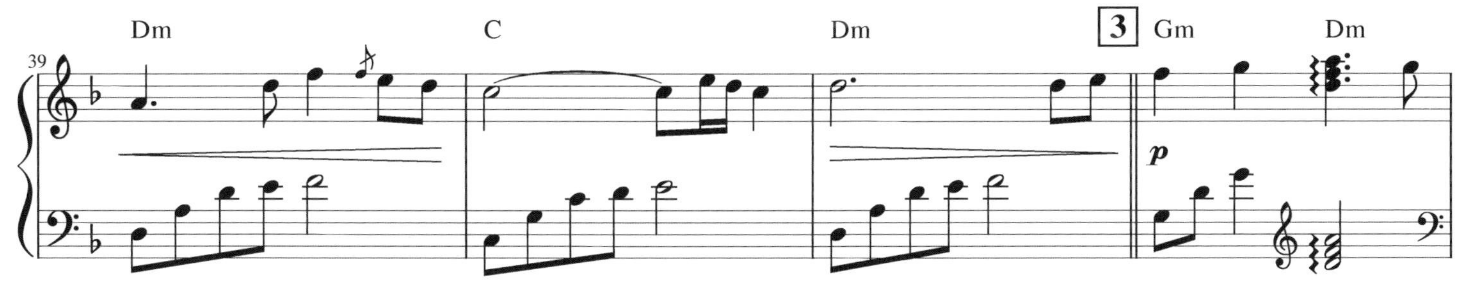
39
Dm
C
Dm
3
Gm
Dm
p

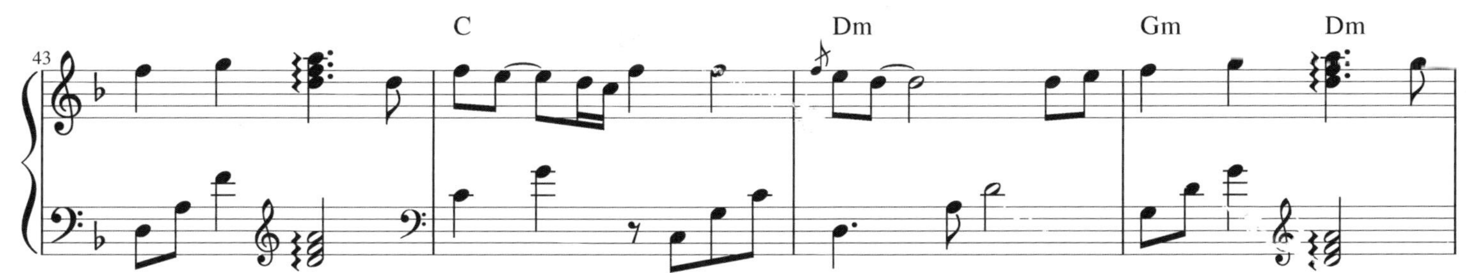
43
C
Dm
Gm
Dm

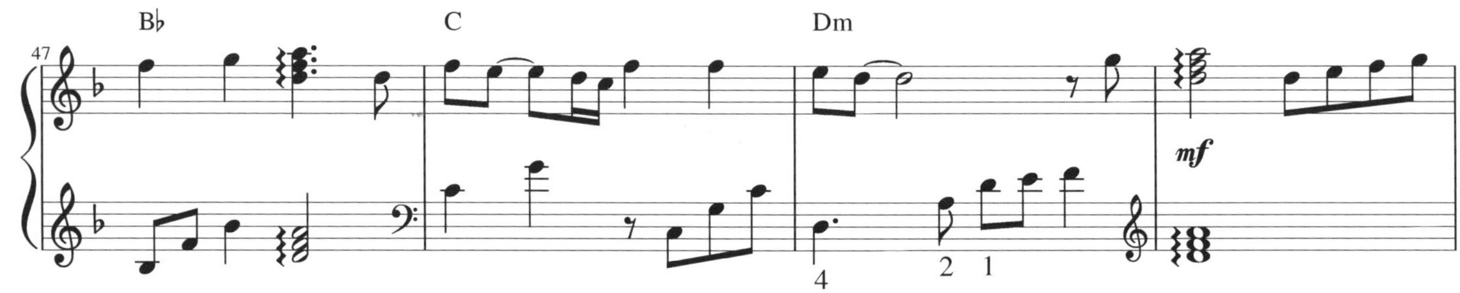
B♭
C
Dm
47
mf
4
2
1

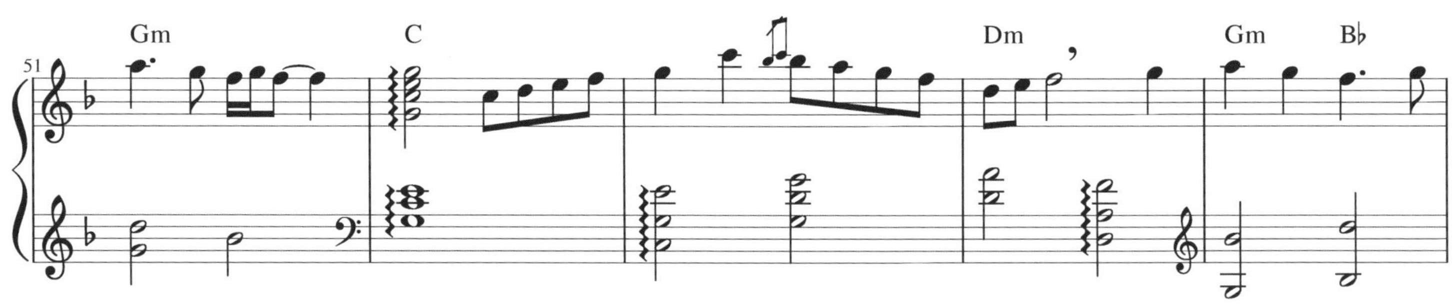
Gm
C
Dm
Gm
B♭
51

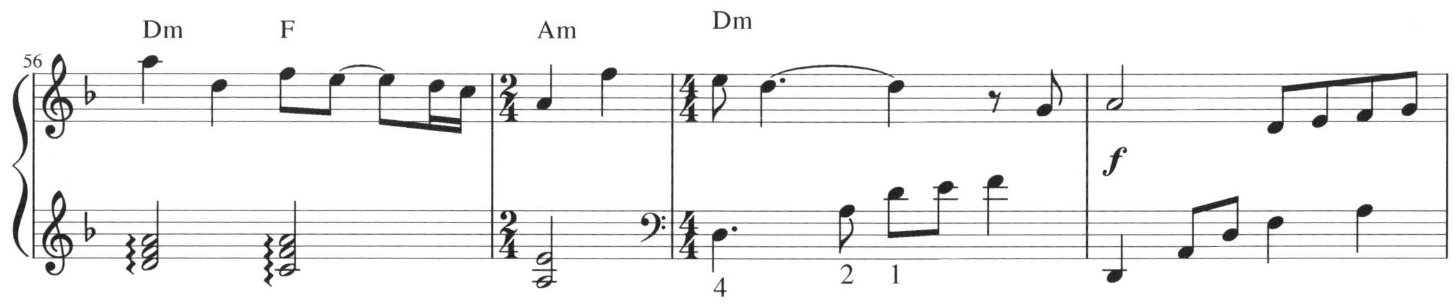
Dm
F
Am
Dm
56
f
4
2
1

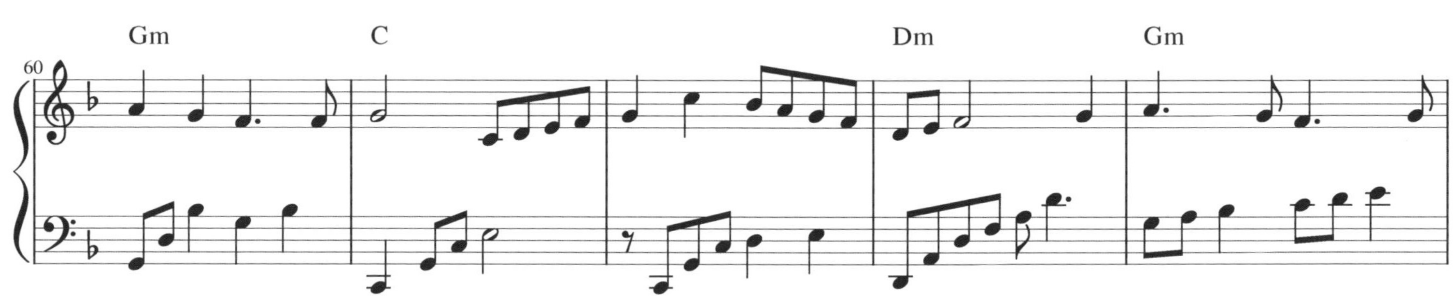
Gm
C
Dm
Gm
60

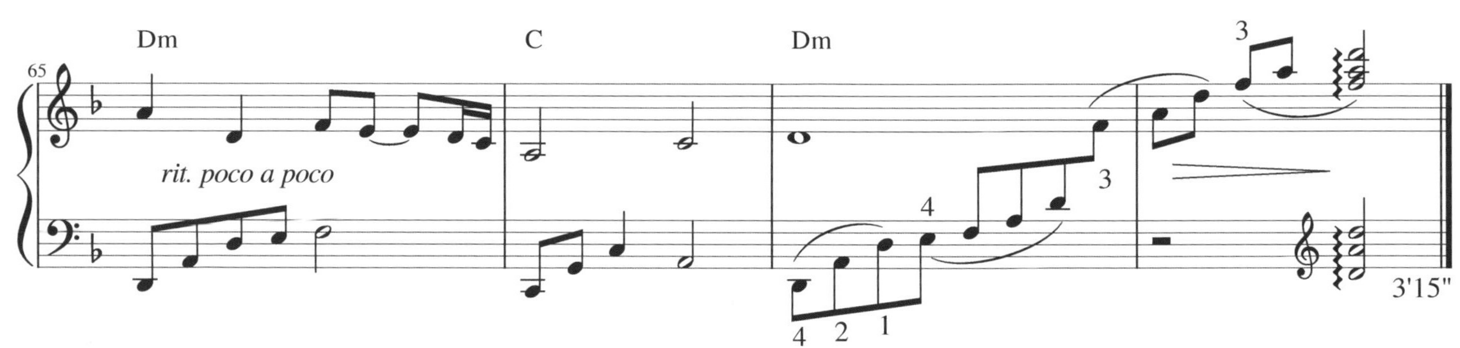
Dm
C
Dm
65
rit. poco a poco
3
4
3
4
2
1
3'15"

Wiggert's Polska

Hambo polska, Traditional Swedish
Arranged by Stephanie Claussen

Carefree, with accents on beat 1

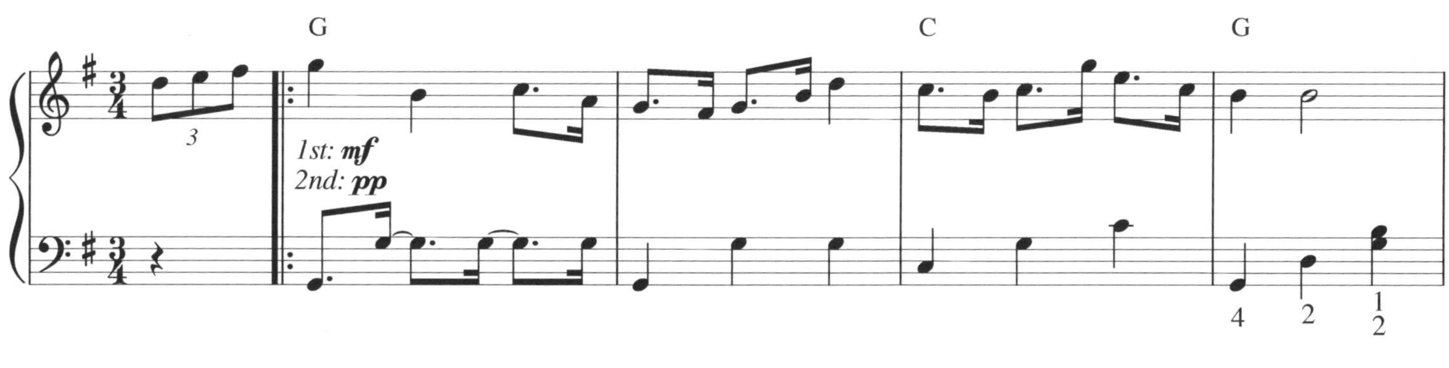

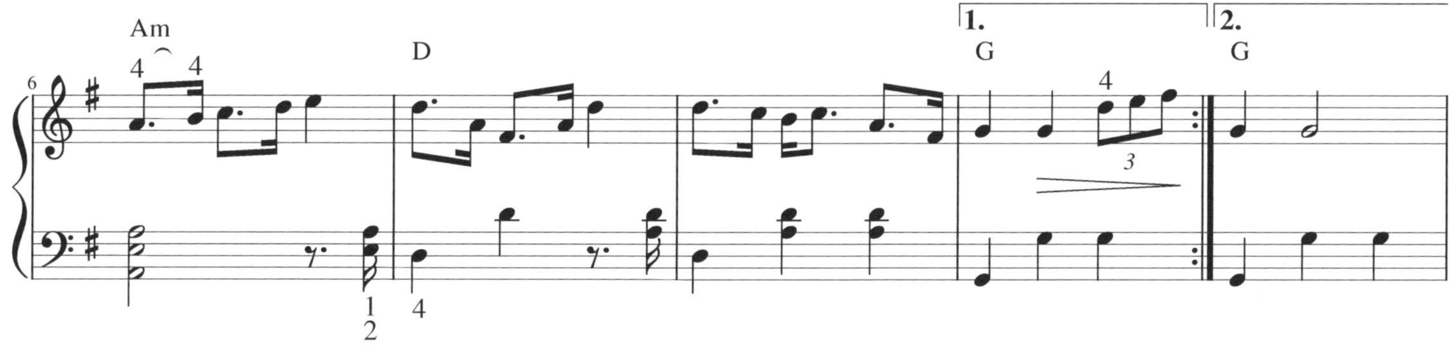

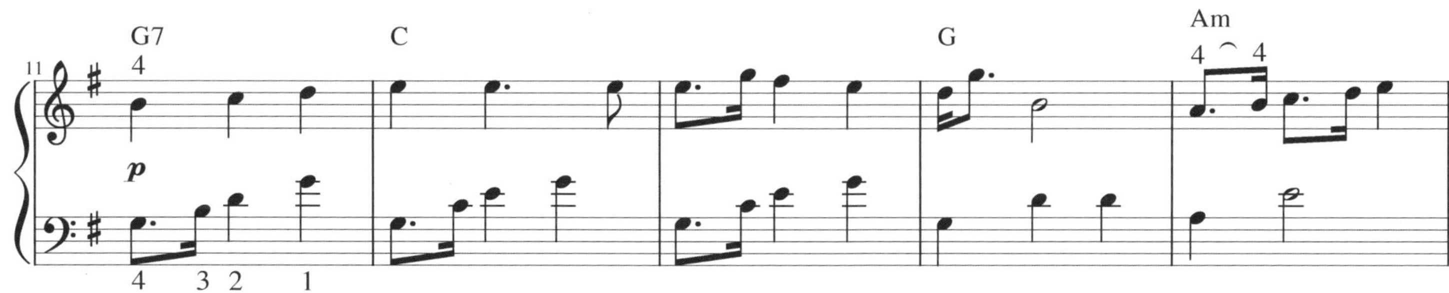

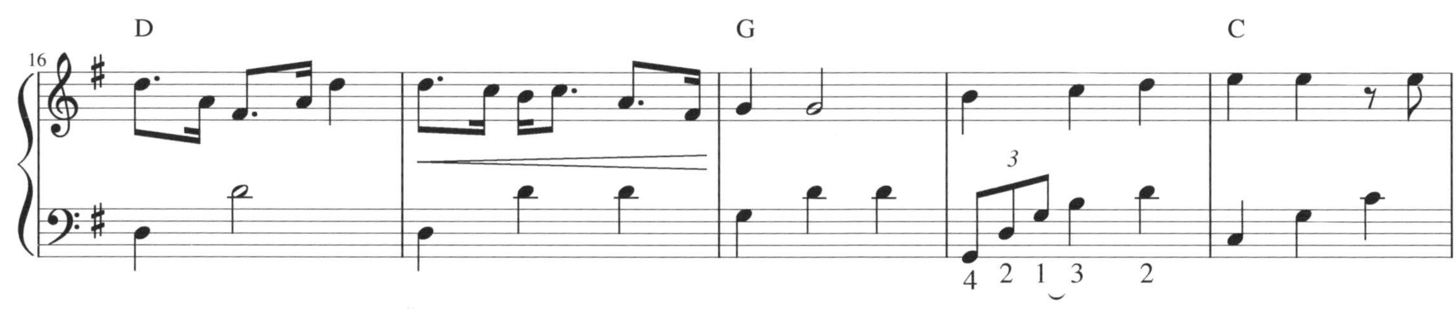

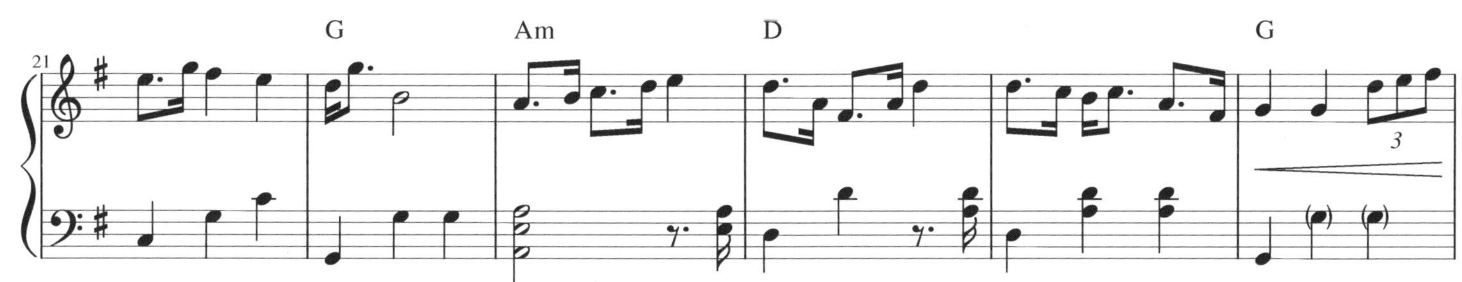

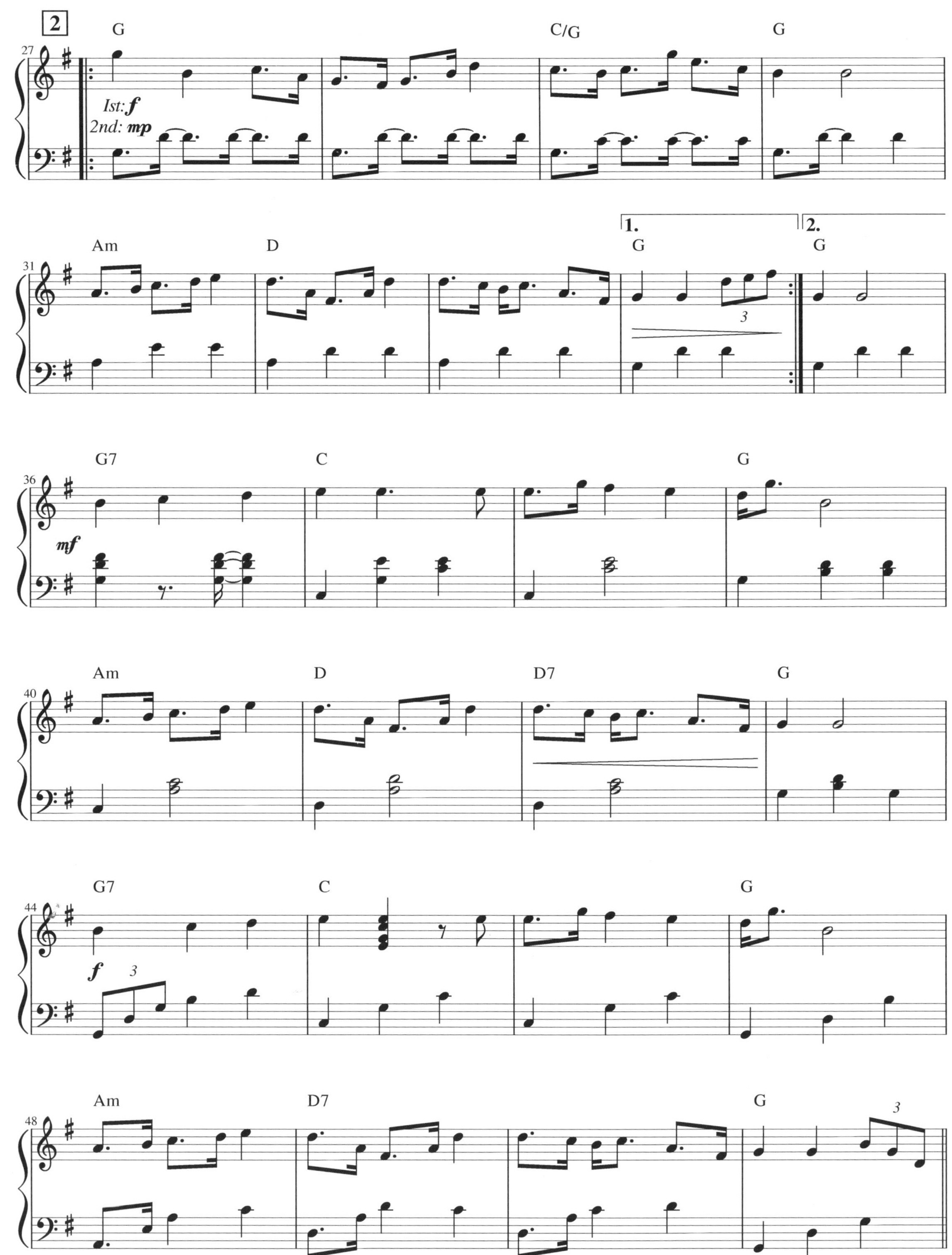
2
G
C/G
G
1st: f
2nd: mp
Am
D
1.
G
2.
G
G7
C
G
mf
Am
D
D7
G
G7
C
G
f
Am
D7
G

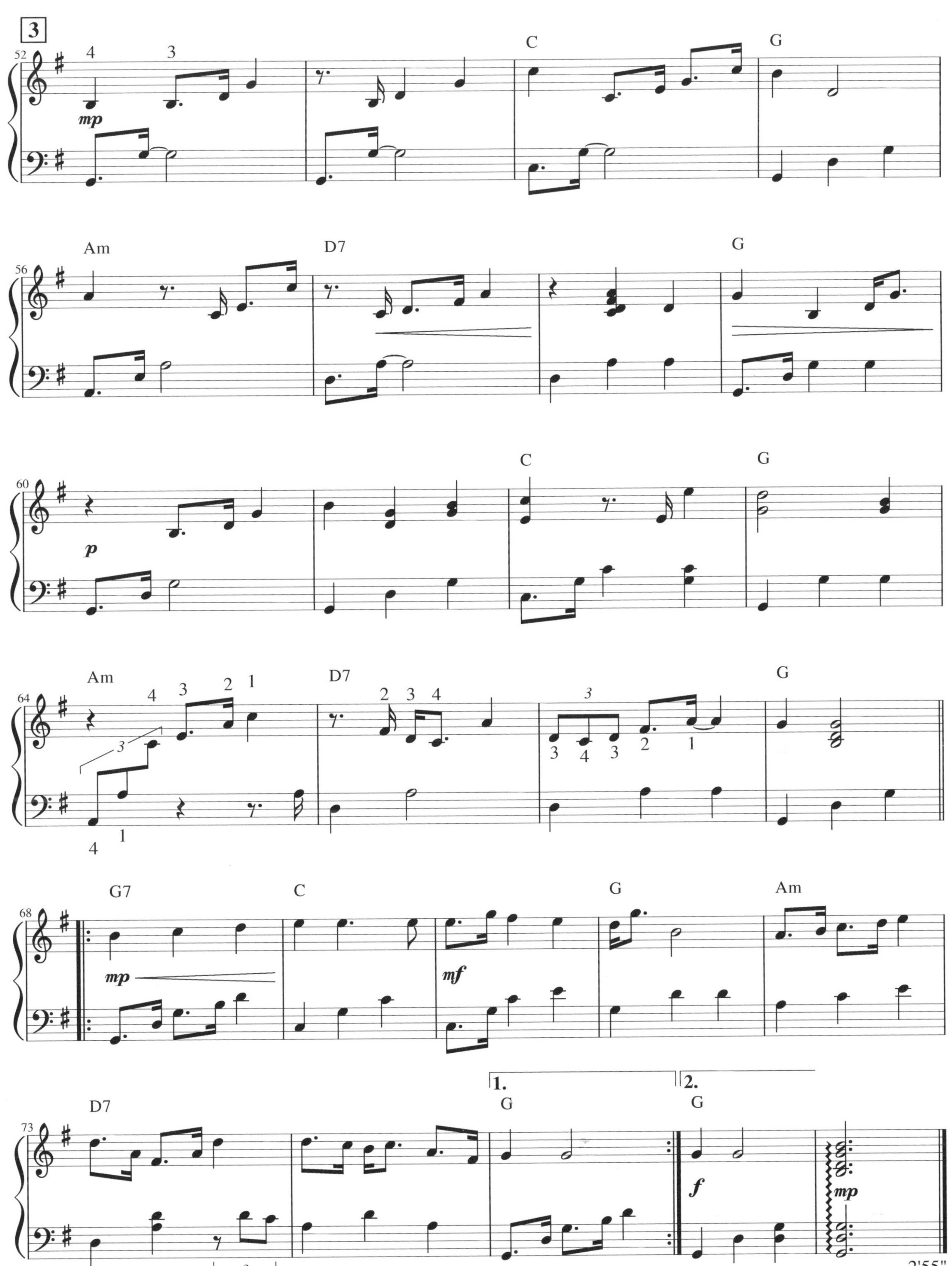
3
52
mp
C
G
56
Am
D7
G
60
p
C
G
64
Am
D7
G
68
G7
mp
C
mf
G
Am
73
D7
1.
G
2.
G
f
mp
2'55"

Cam Ye O'er Frae France

Traditional Scottish
Arranged by Stephanie Claussen

Brisk and rollicking

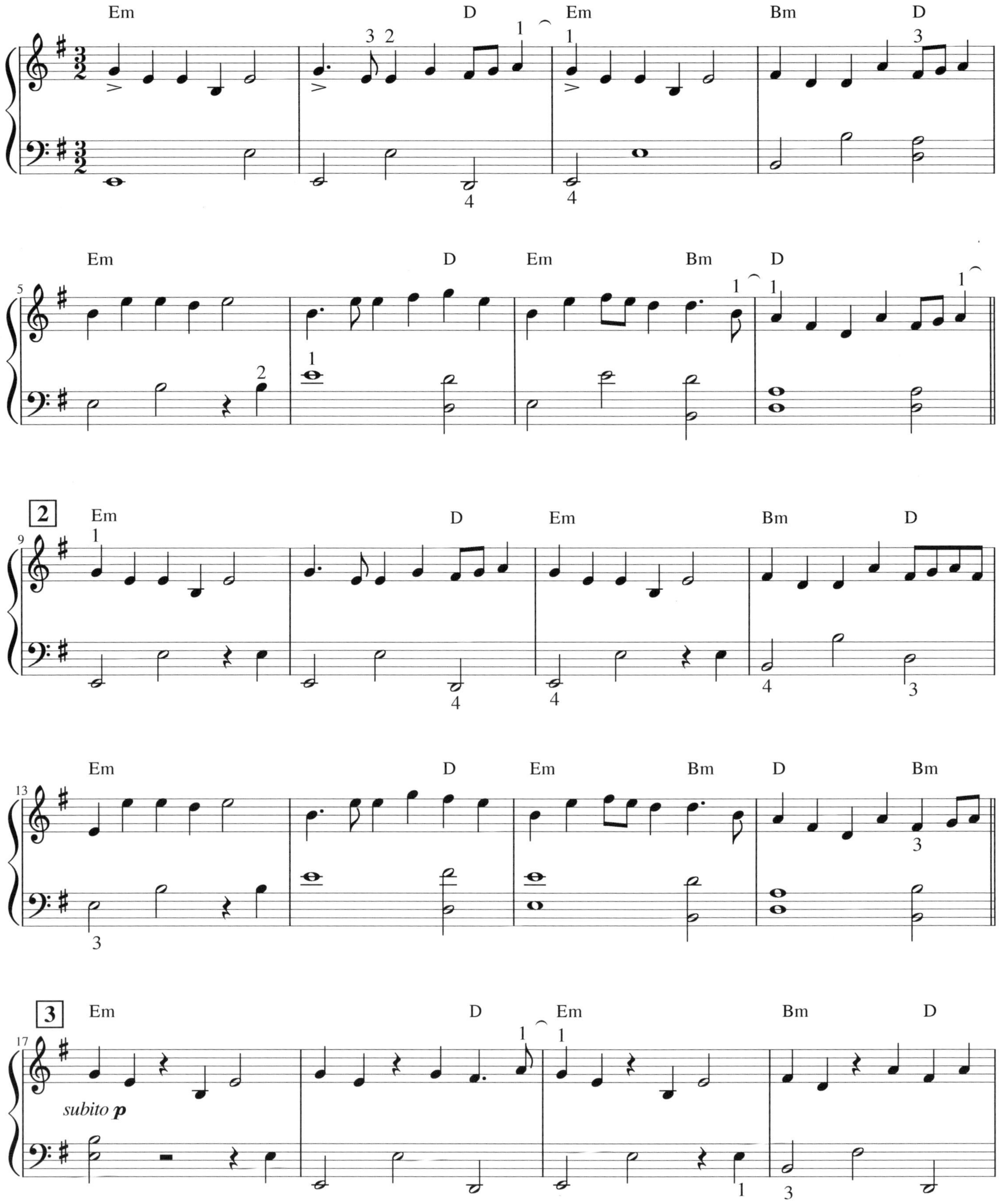

subito ***p***

All left-hand octaves, broken or otherwise, should be played flat.

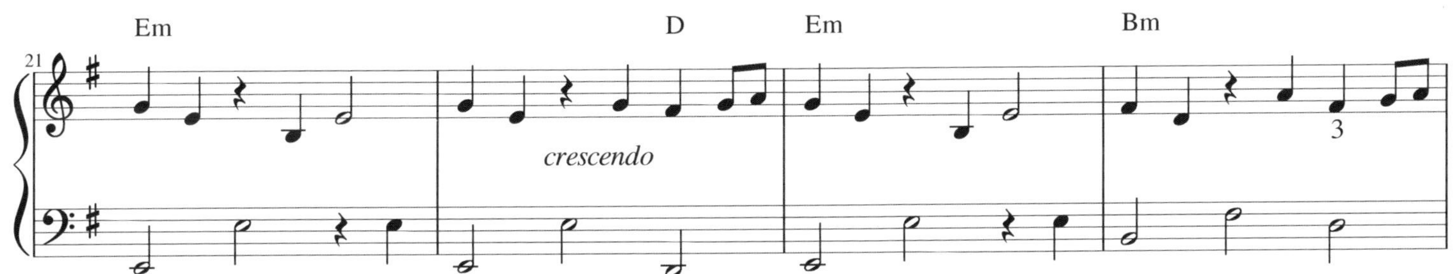
Em
D
Em
Bm
21
crescendo
3

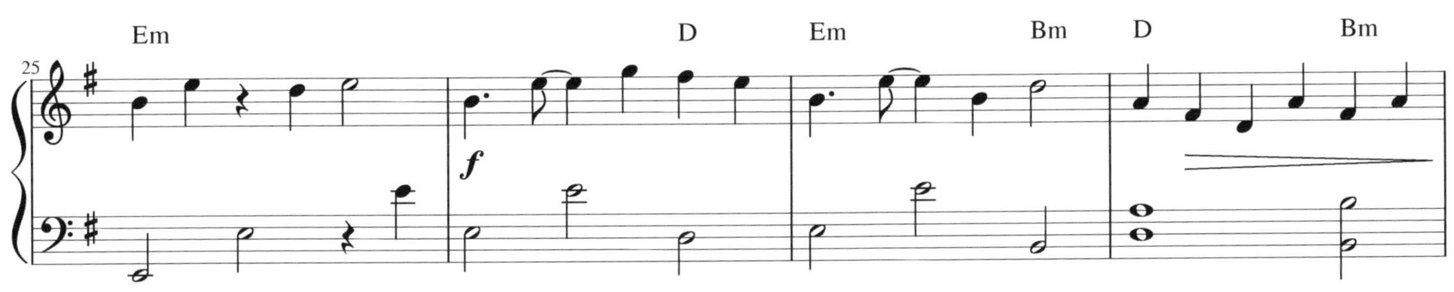
Em
D
Em
Bm
D
Bm
25
f

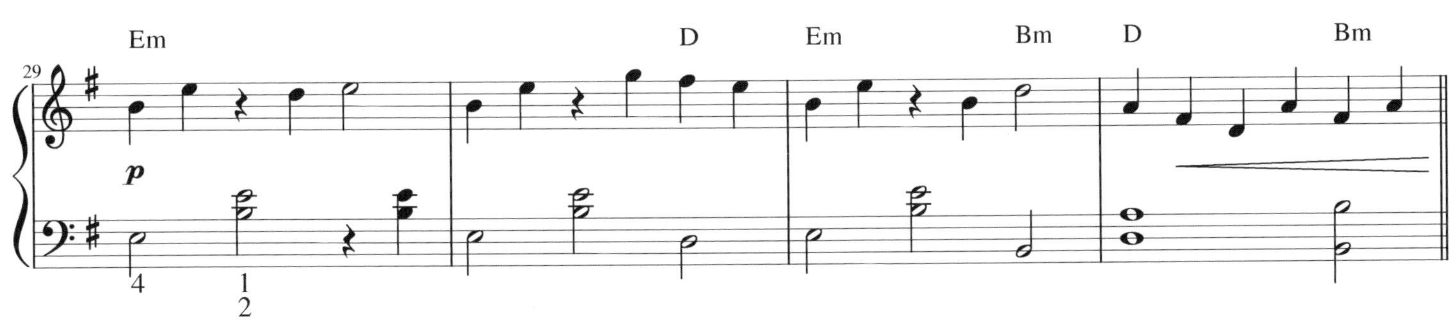
Em
D
Em
Bm
D
Bm
29
p
4
1
2

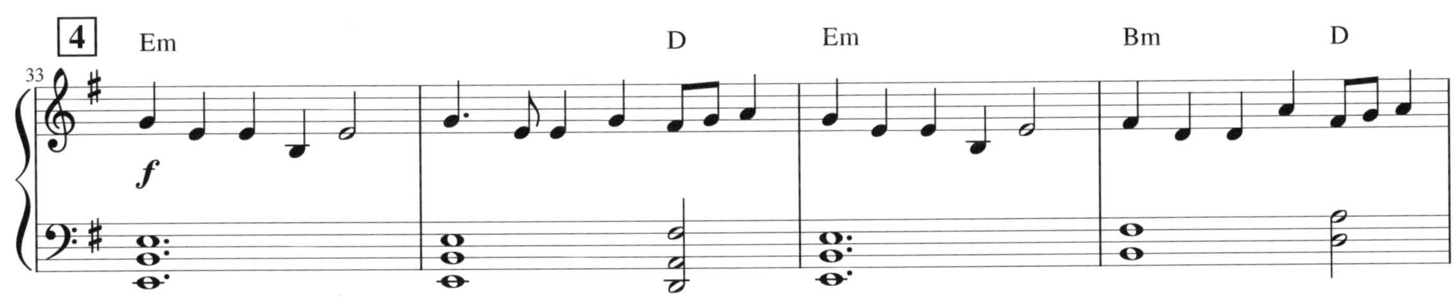
4
Em
D
Em
Bm
D
33
f

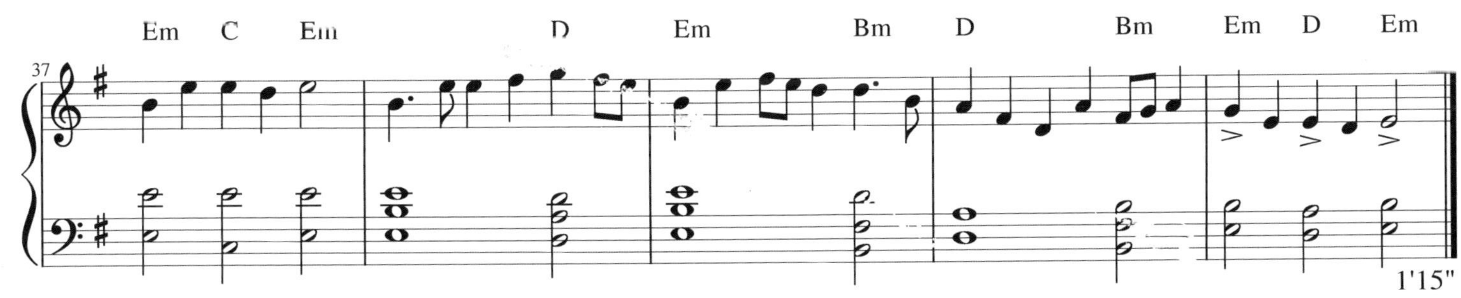
Em
C
Em
D
Em
Bm
D
Bm
Em
D
Em
37
1'15"

To Daunton Me

Bold and arrogant
Set the middle C♯ and the C♯ one octave above it.

Strathspey, Traditional Scottish
Arranged by Stephanie Claussen

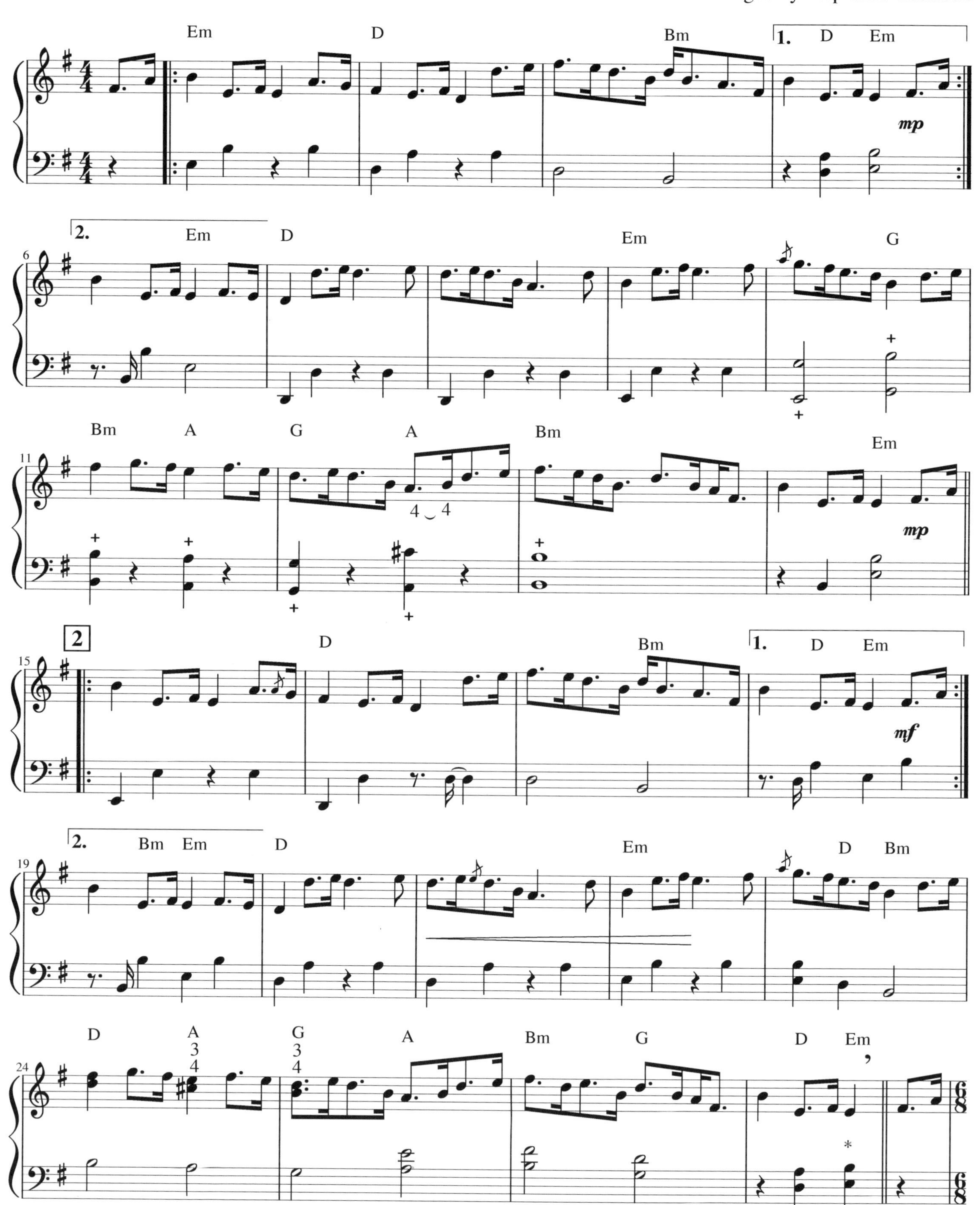

* If ending here, substitute a low E octave in the bass.

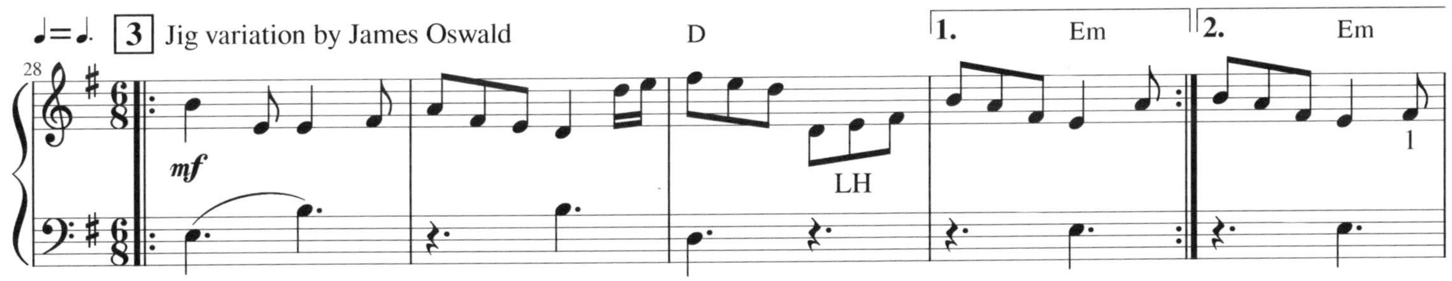

♩=♩.
3
Jig variation by James Oswald
28
mf
D
LH
1.
Em
2.
Em

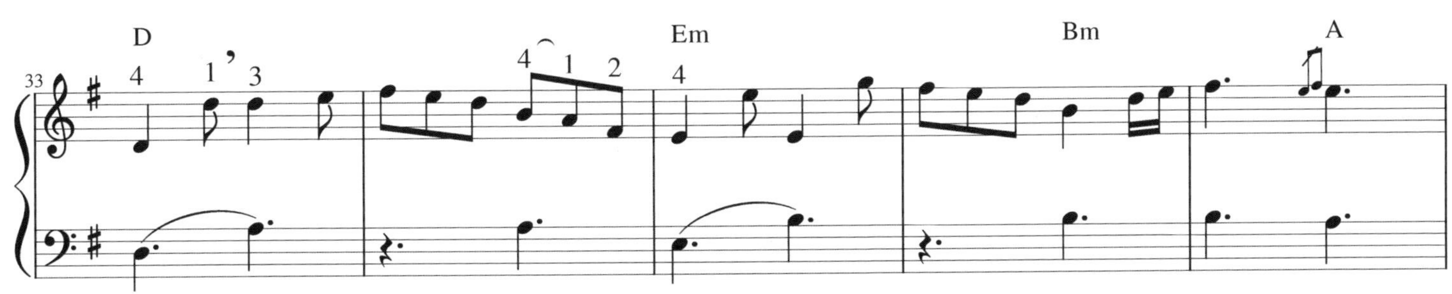

33
D
Em
Bm
A

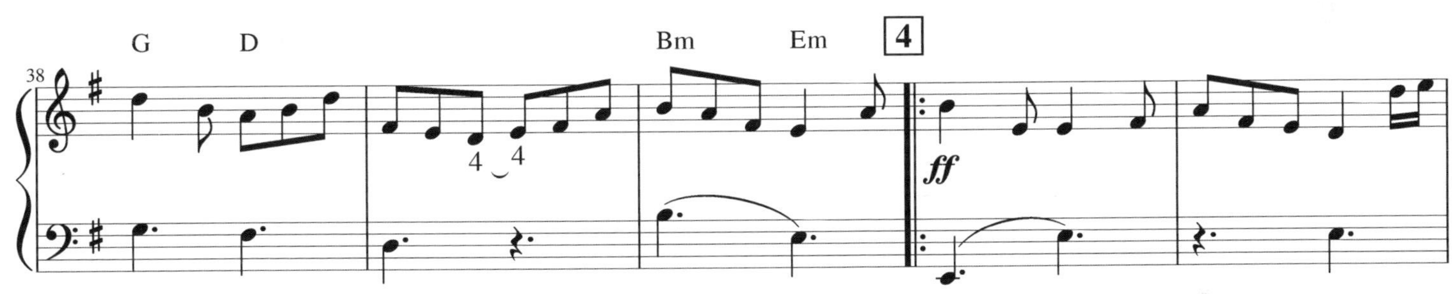

38
G
D
Bm
Em
4
ff

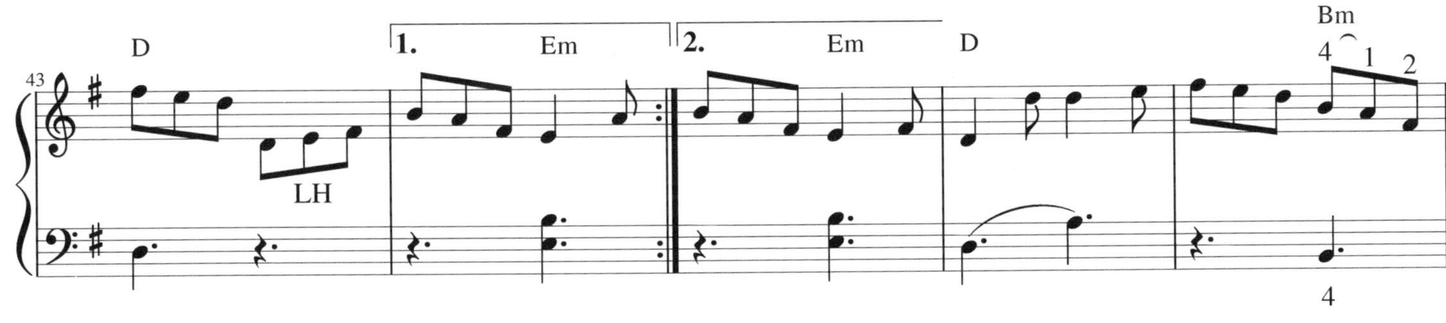

43
D
LH
1.
Em
2.
Em
D
Bm

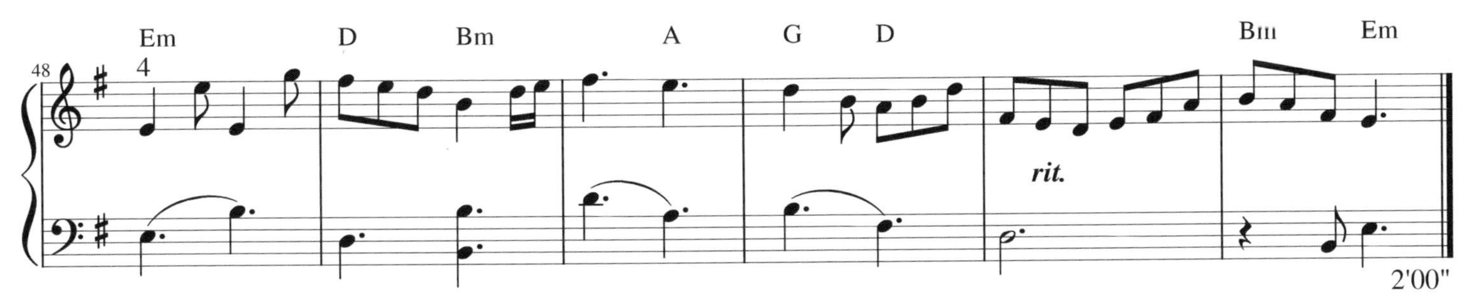

48
Em
D
Bm
A
G
D
rit.
Bm
Em
2'00"

Ca' The Yowes to the Knowes

Air, Traditional Scottish
Arranged by Stephanie Claussen

Peaceful but powerful

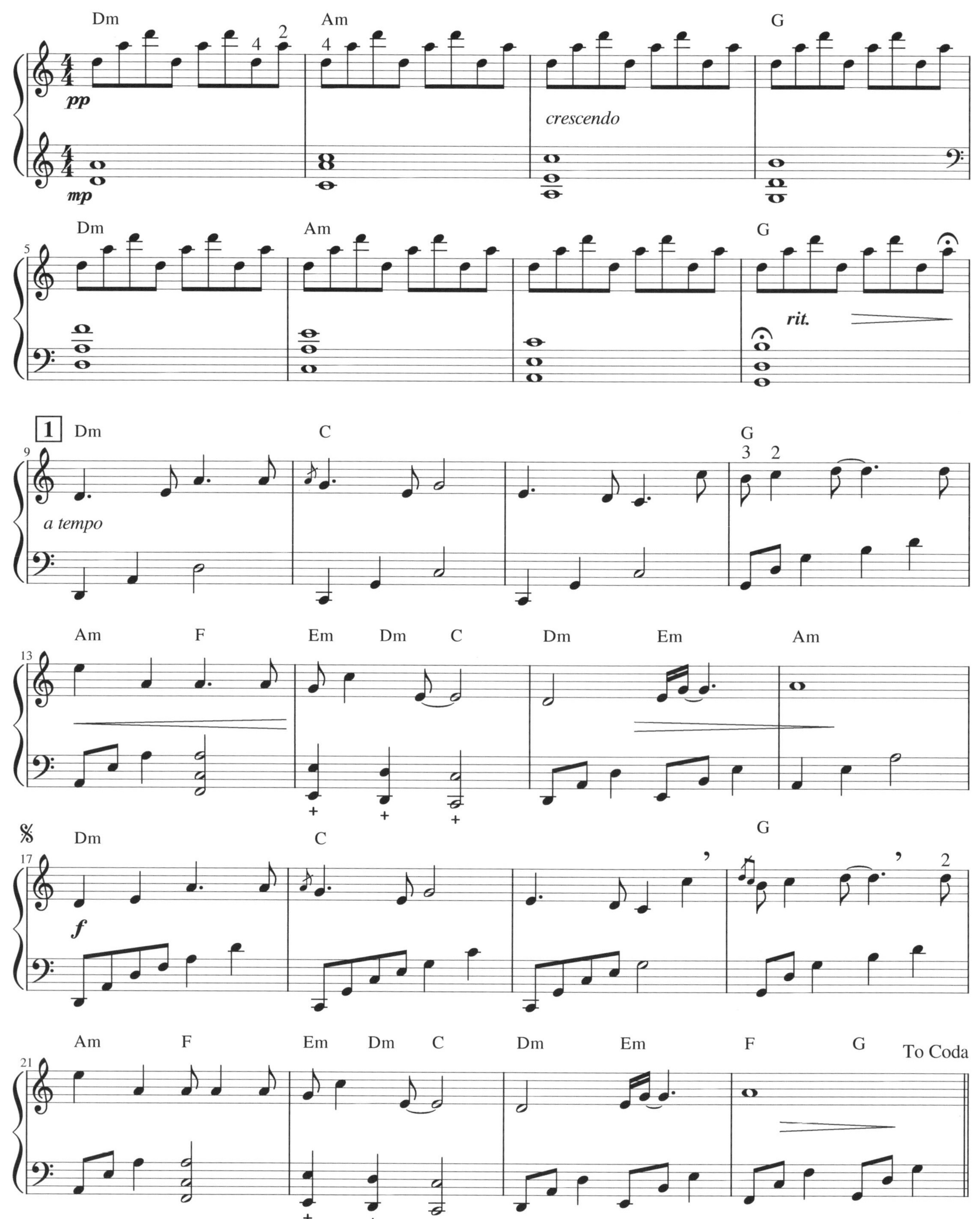

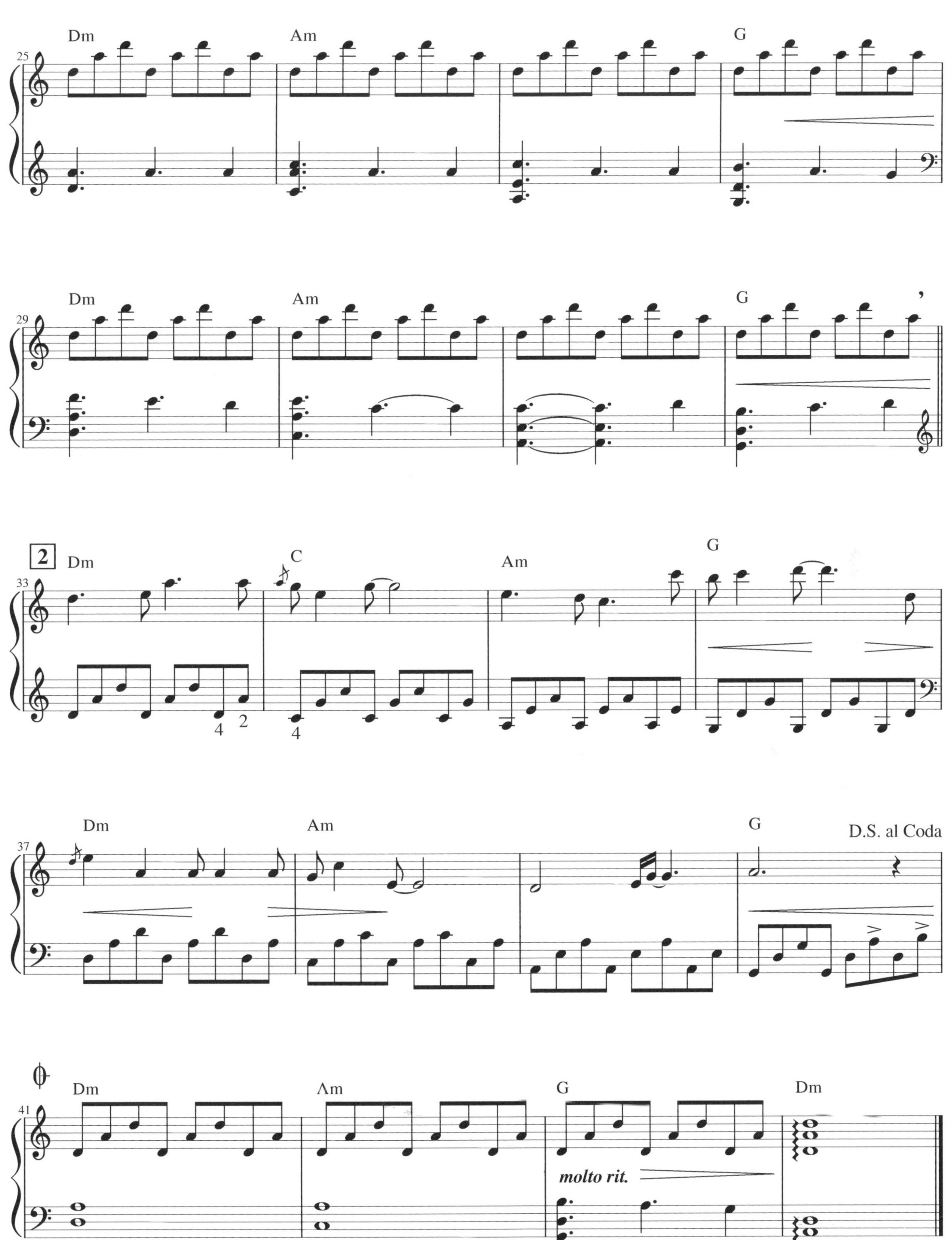
Dm
Am
G
Dm
Am
G
2
Dm
C
Am
G
Dm
Am
G
D.S. al Coda
Dm
Am
G
Dm
molto rit.
2'30"

Morpeth Lasses

With attitude, but not too fast

Reel, Traditional Scottish
Arranged by Stephanie Claussen

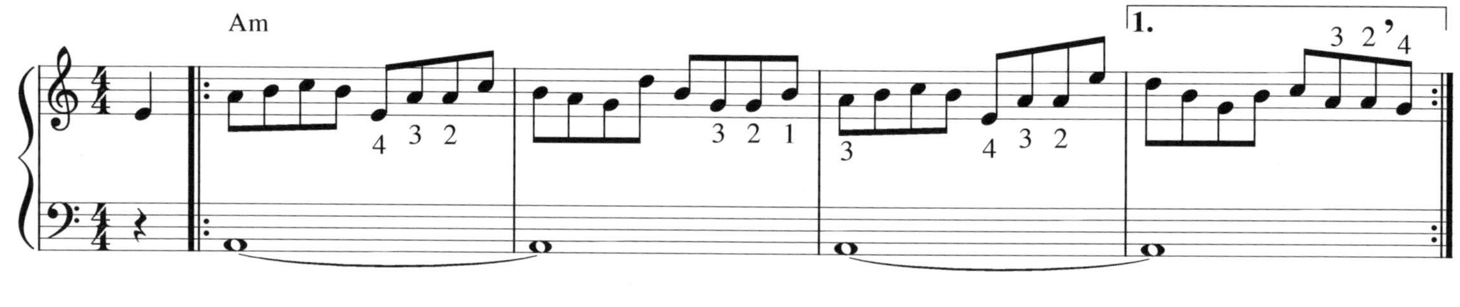

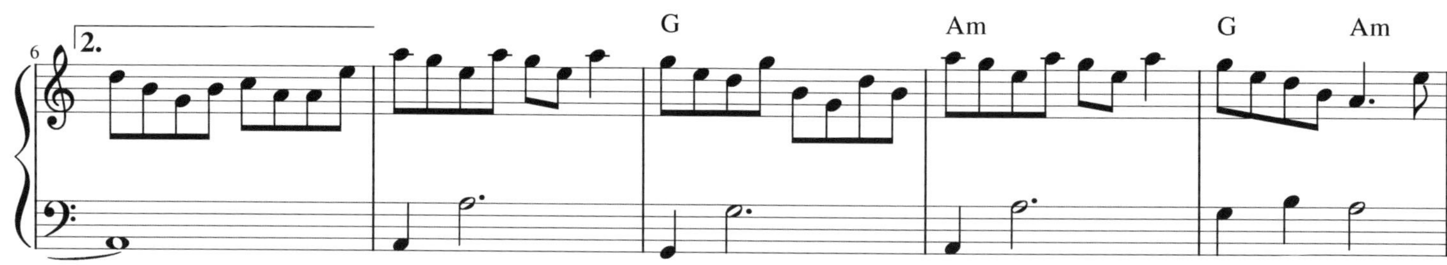

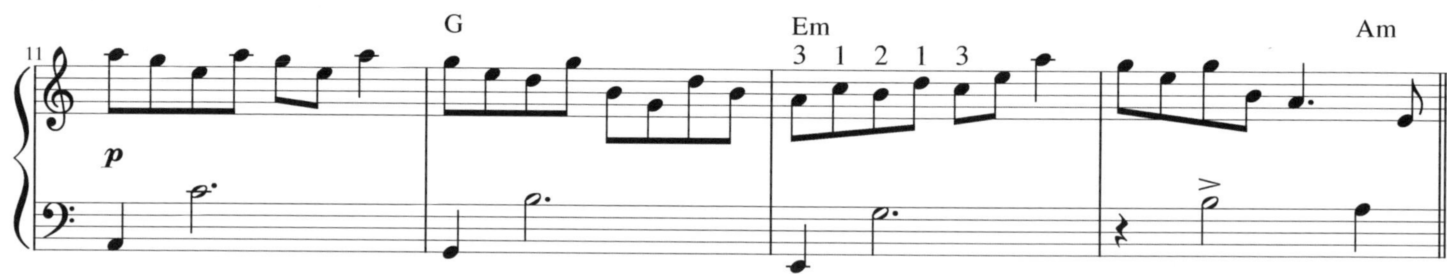

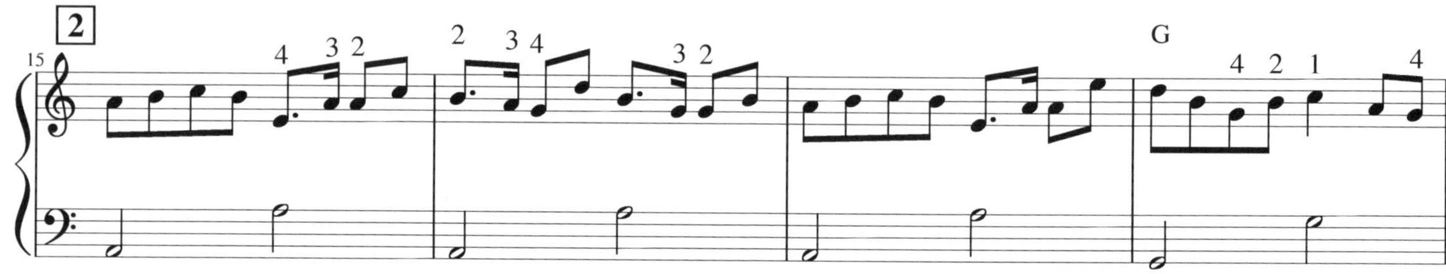

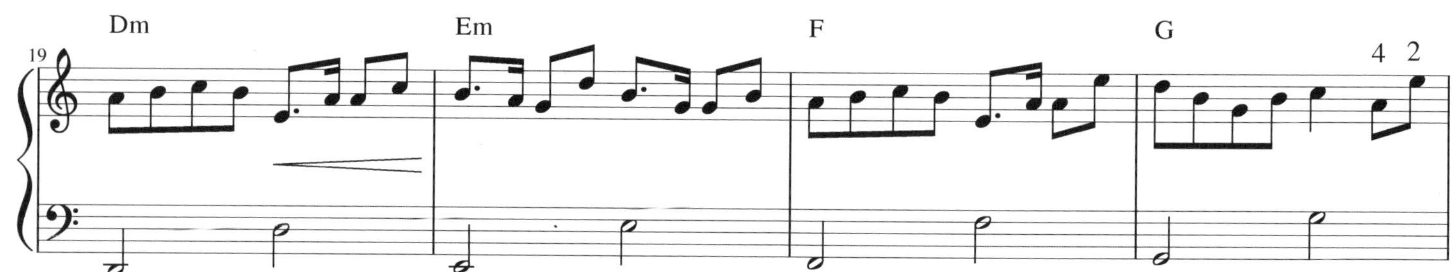

All left-hand octaves, 9ths, and 10ths, broken or otherwise, should be played flat.

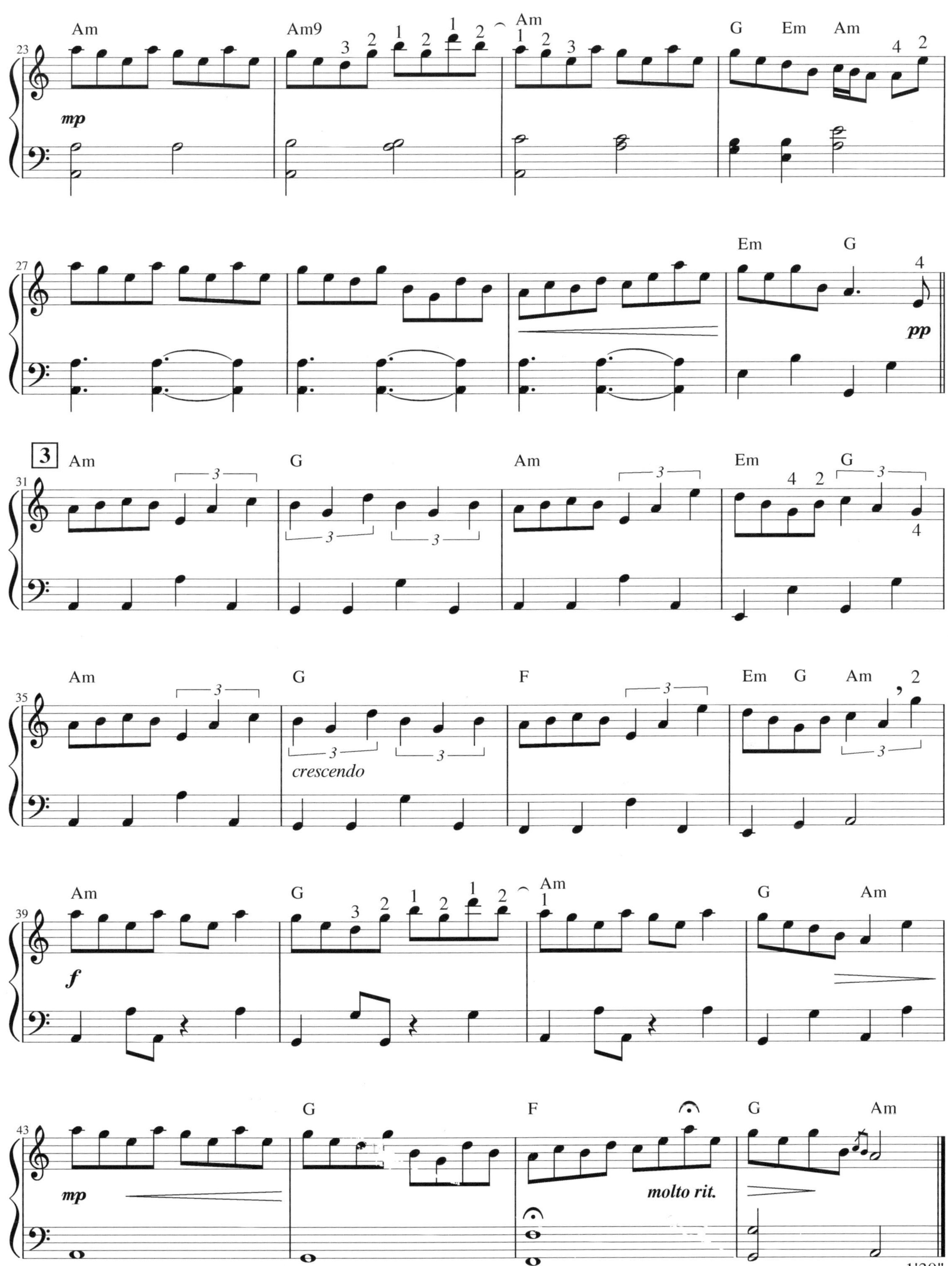
Am Am9 Am G Em Am
mp
Em G
pp
Am G Am Em G
Am G F Em G Am
crescendo
Am G Am G Am
f
G F G Am
mp
molto rit.
1'30"

Small is my Inclination to Sleep

Air, Traditional Scottish
Arranged by Stephanie Claussen

Very slow and plaintive

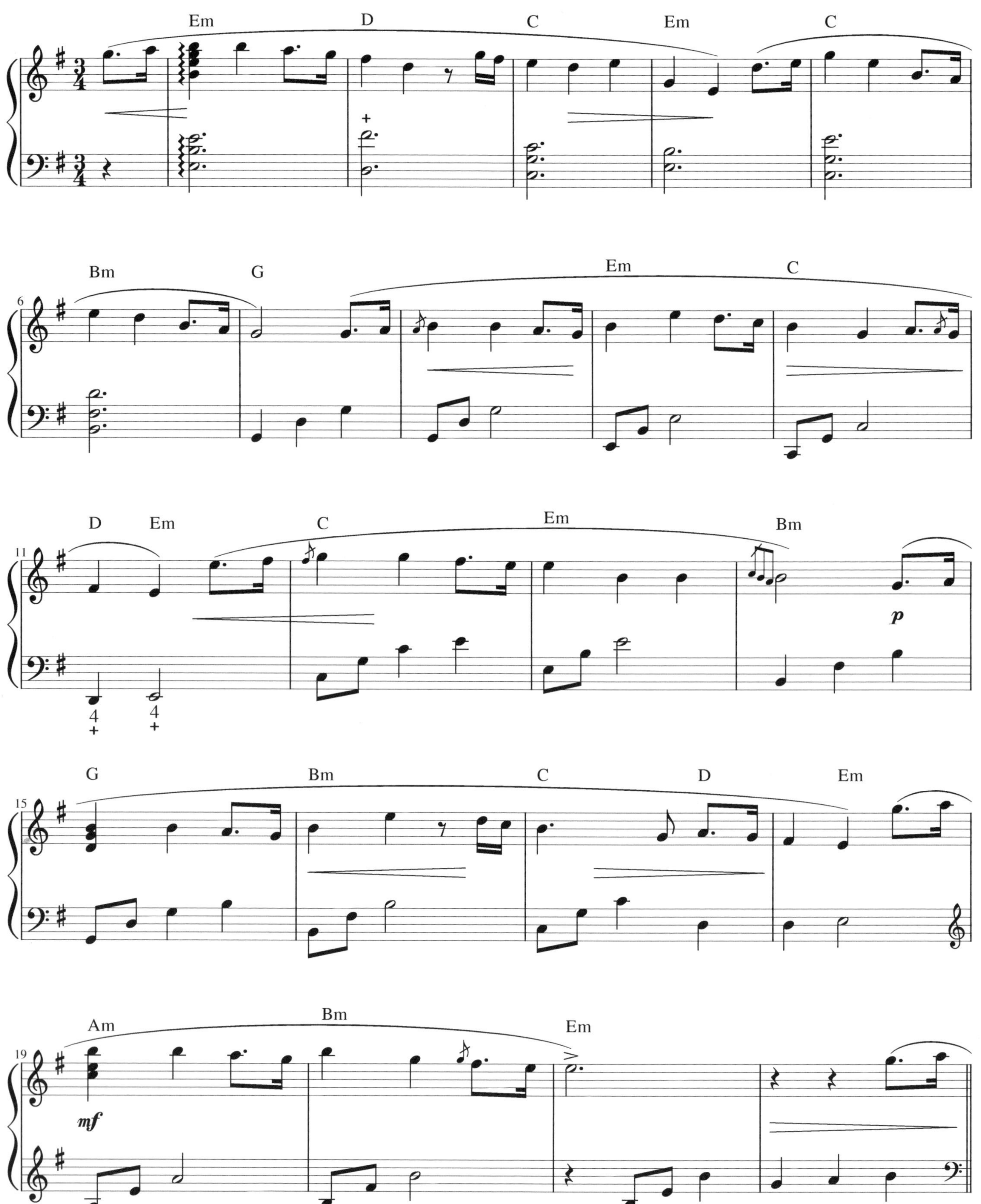

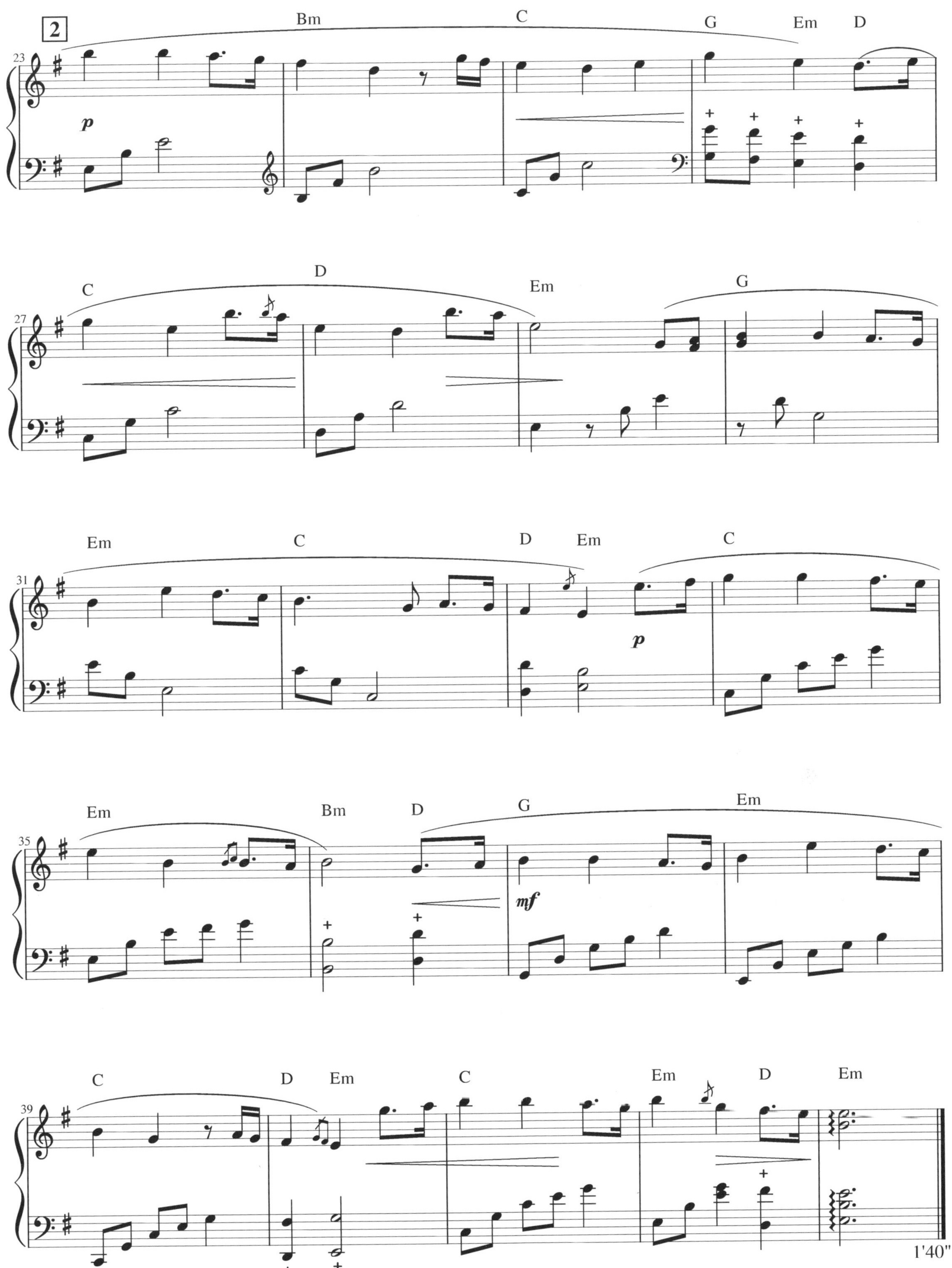
2
Bm
C
G
Em
D
p
C
D
Em
G
Em
C
D
Em
C
p
Em
Bm
D
G
Em
mf
C
D
Em
C
Em
D
Em
1'40"

The Duke of Fife's Welcome to Deeside

Scottish March

by James Scott Skinner
Arranged by Stephanie Claussen

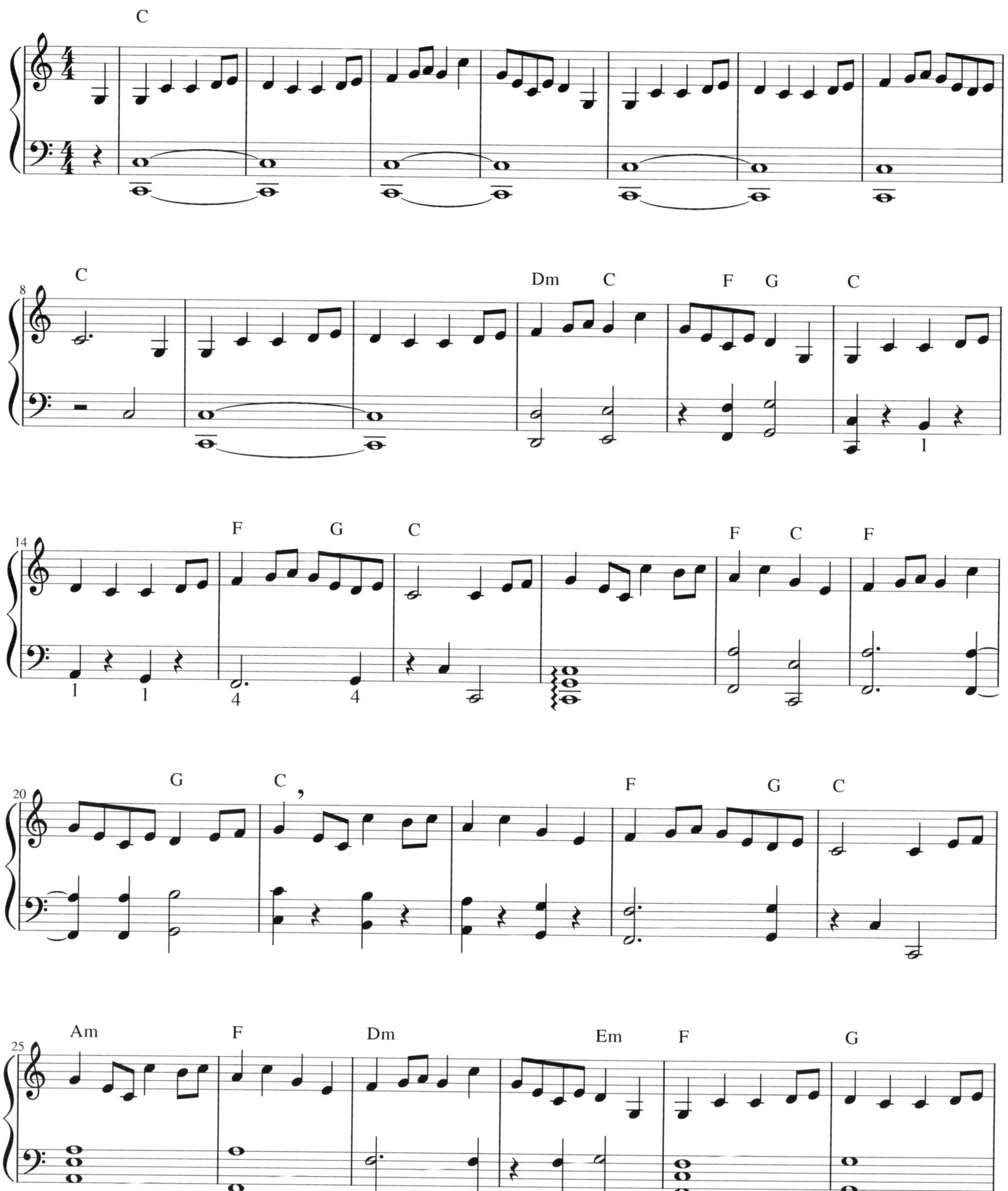

All left-hand octaves and 10ths, broken or otherwise, should be played flat.

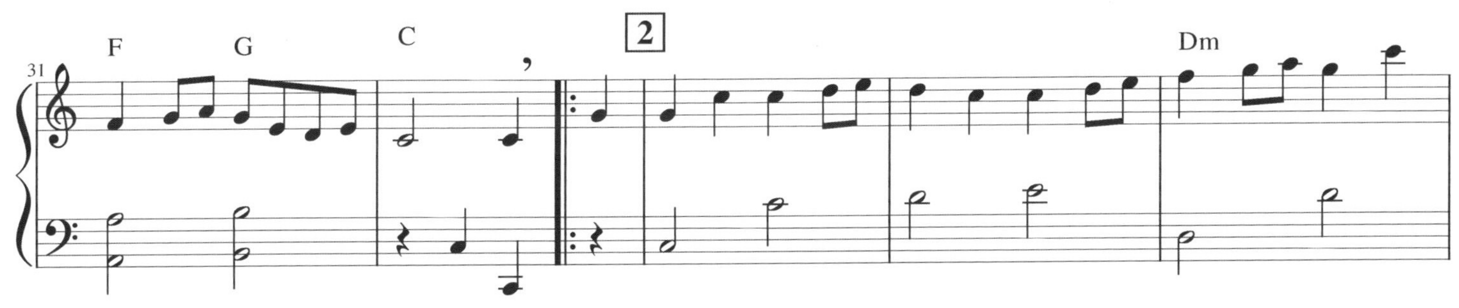
31
F
G
C
2
Dm

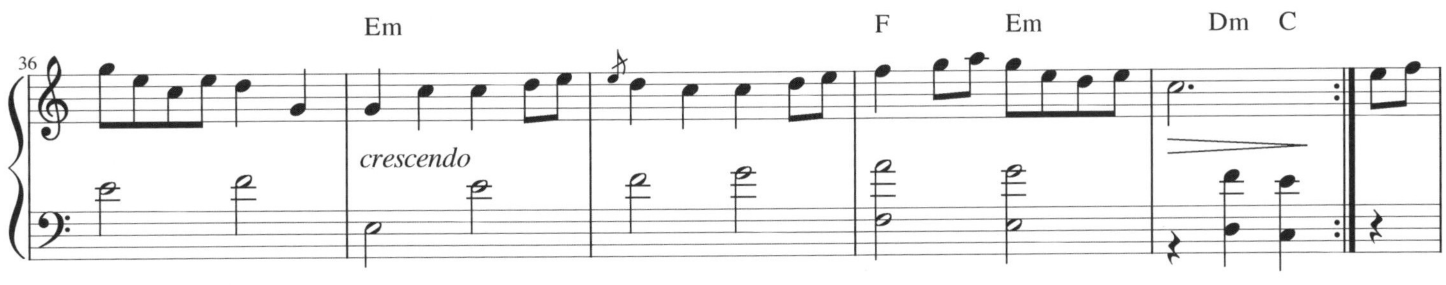
36
Em
crescendo
F
Em
Dm
C

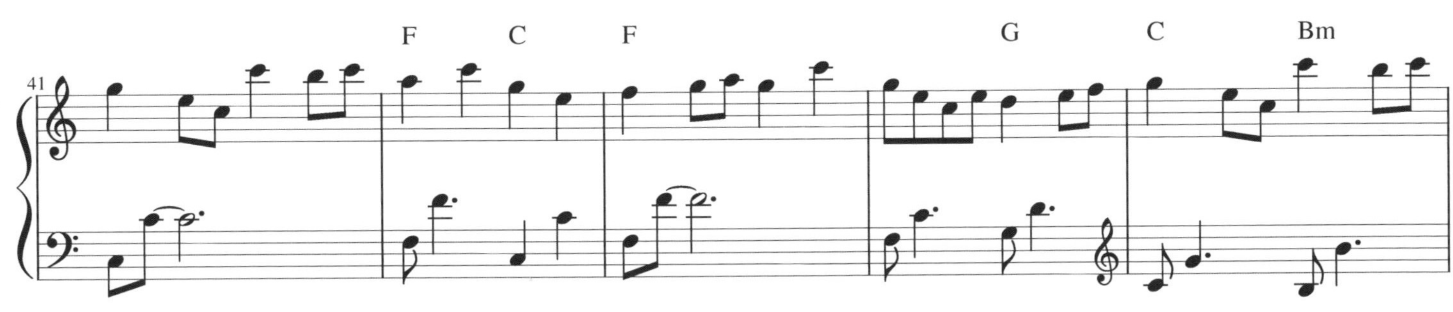
41
F
C
F
G
C
Bm

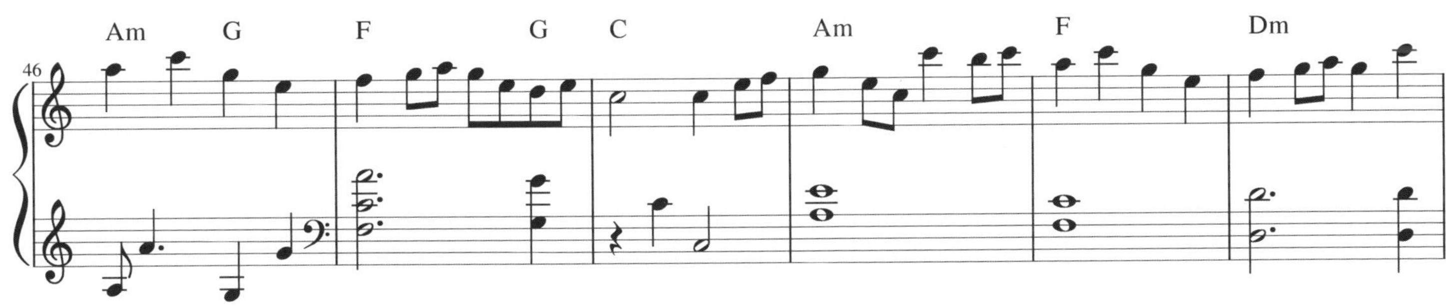
46
Am
G
F
G
C
Am
F
Dm

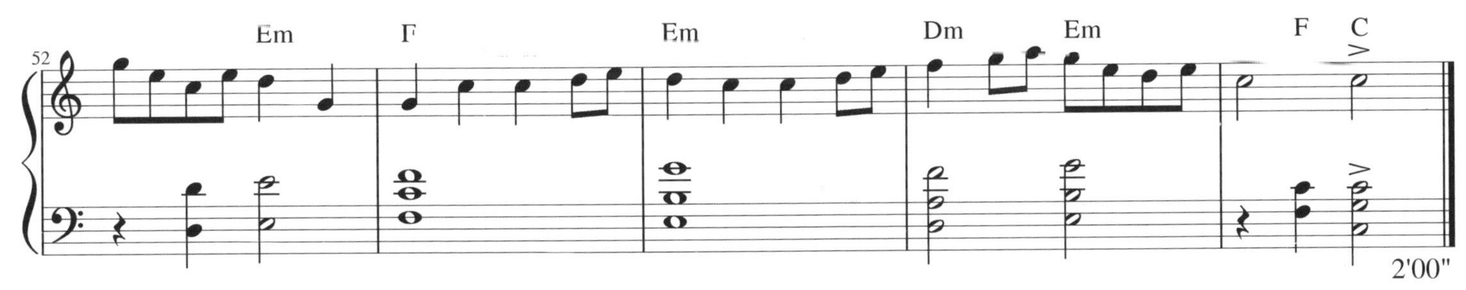
52
Em
F
Em
Dm
Em
F
C
2'00"

The Greenwood Side

March, Traditional Scottish
Arranged by Stephanie Claussen

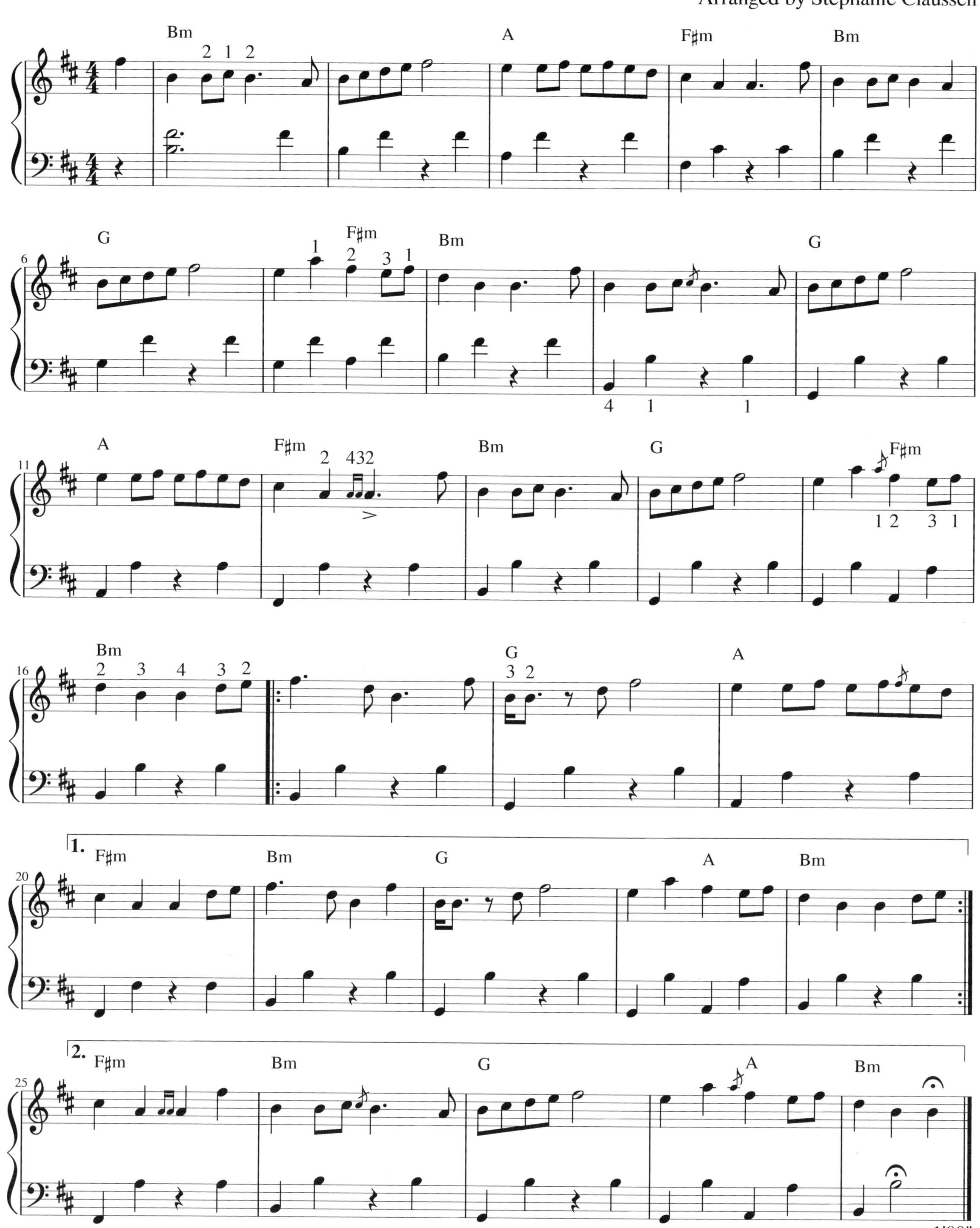

All left-hand octaves, broken or otherwise, should be played flat.

Campbell's Farewell to Redcastle

March, Traditional Scottish
Arranged by Stephanie Claussen

Brisk

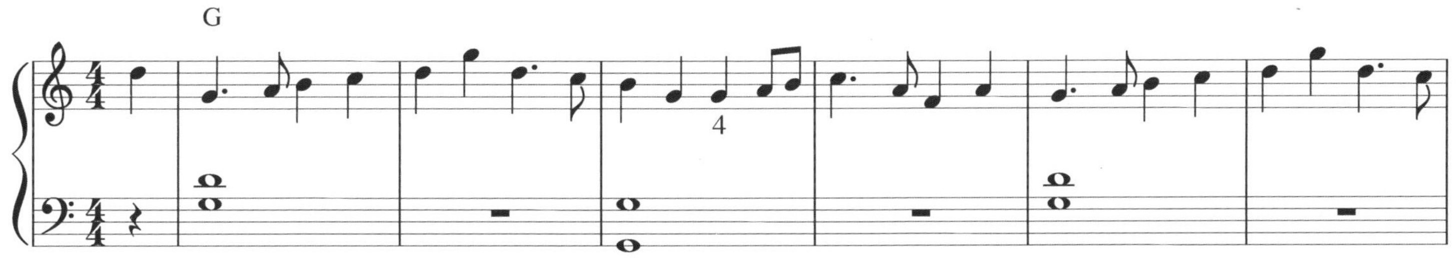

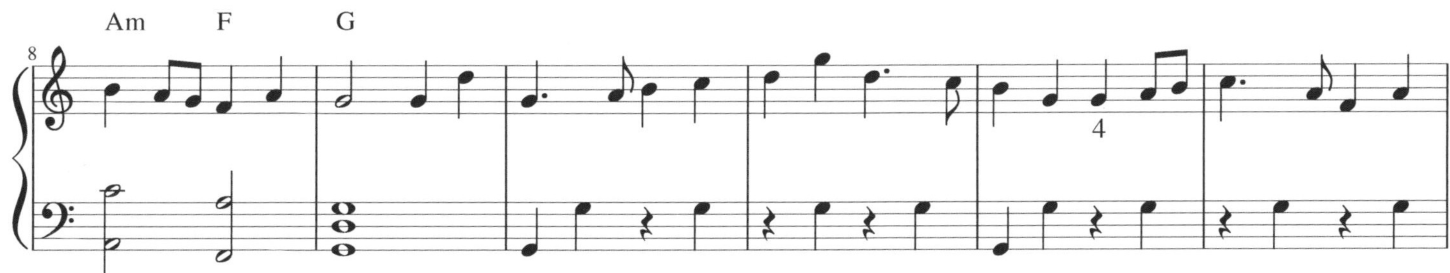

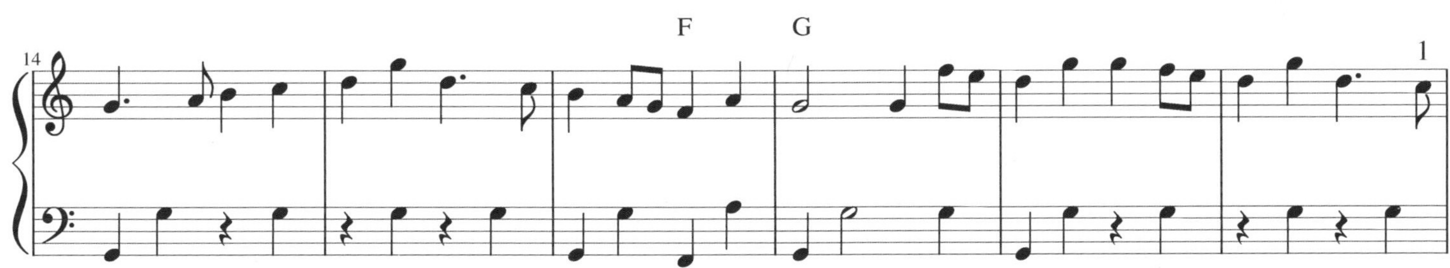

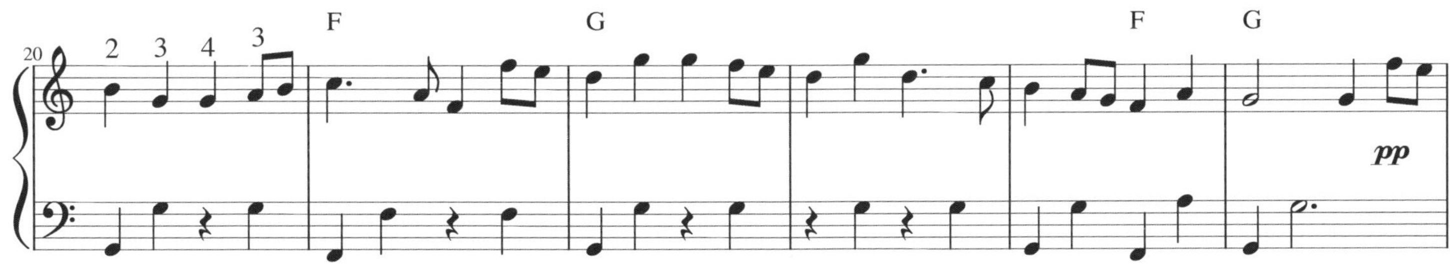

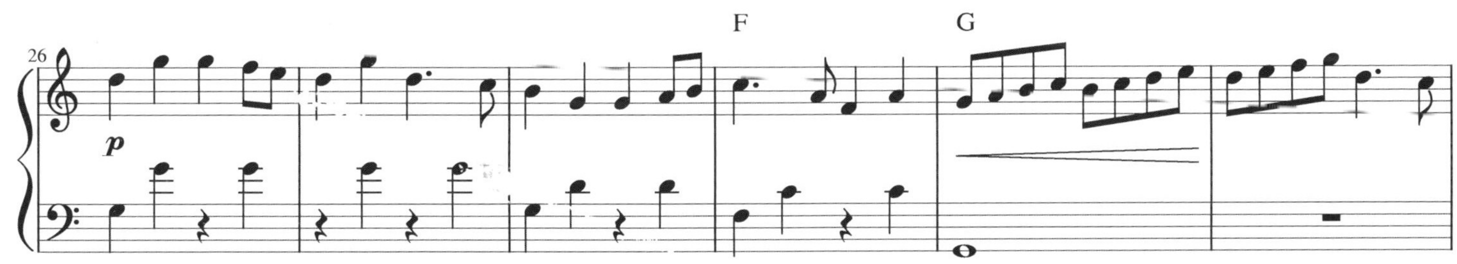

All left-hand octaves, broken or otherwise, should be played flat.

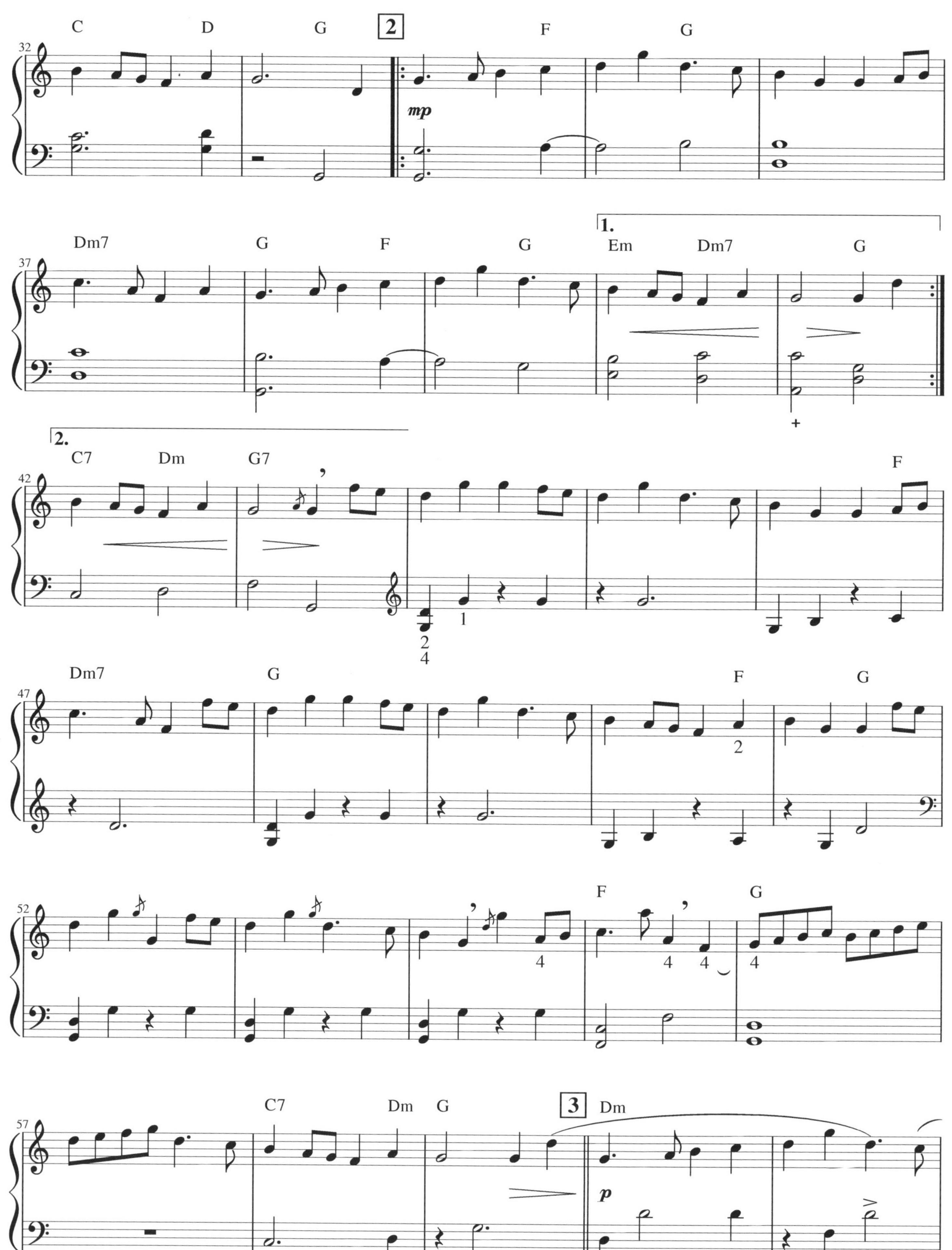
C D G
2
F G
mp
Dm7 G F G
1.
Em Dm7 G
2.
C7 Dm G7
F
Dm7 G F G
F G
C7 Dm G
3
Dm
p

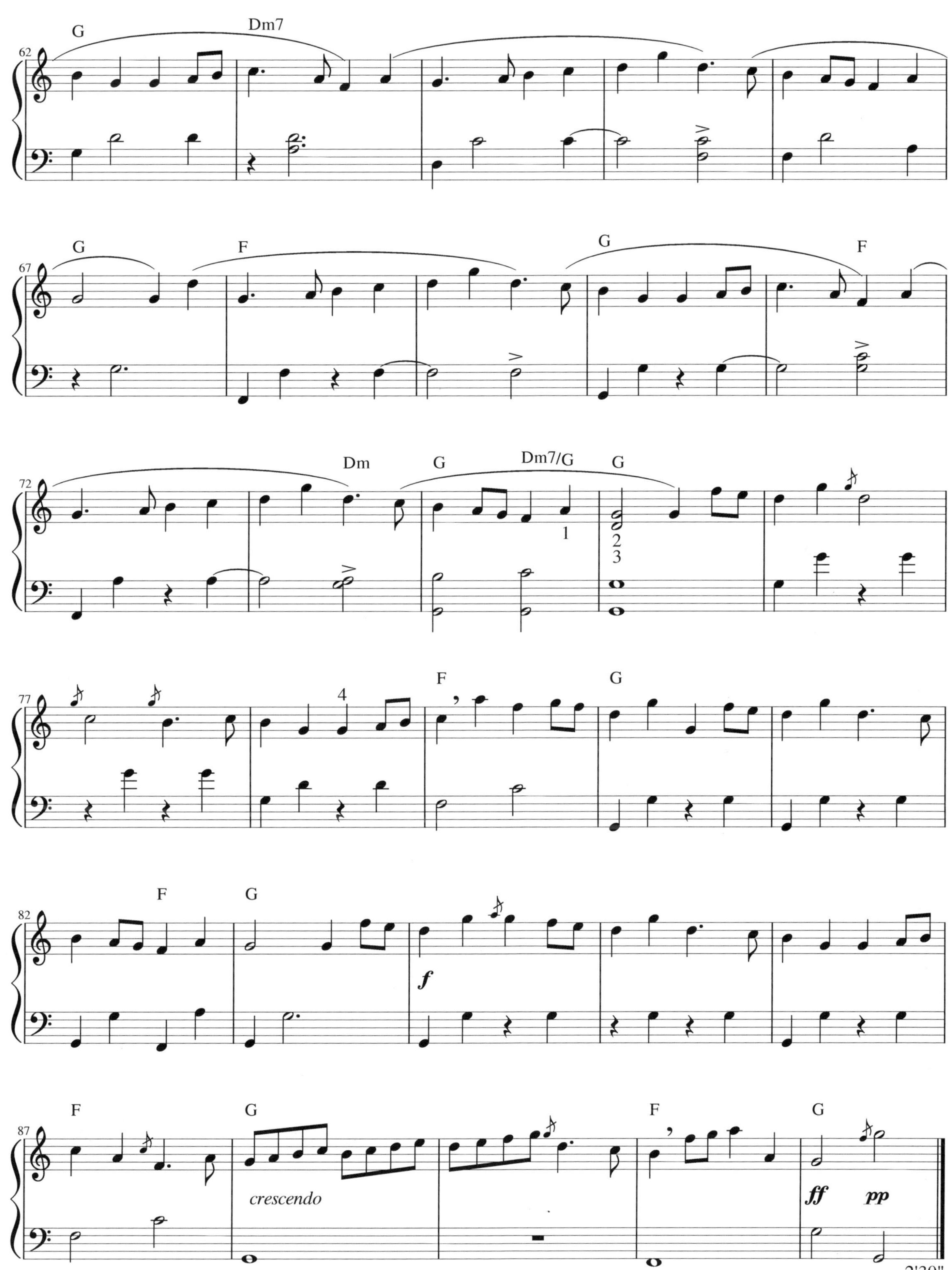
G
Dm7
G
F
G
F
Dm
G
Dm7/G
G
F
G
F
G
f
F
G
crescendo
F
G
ff
pp
2'30"

Loch Ruthven

Strathspey, Traditional Scottish
Arranged by Stephanie Claussen

With vigor

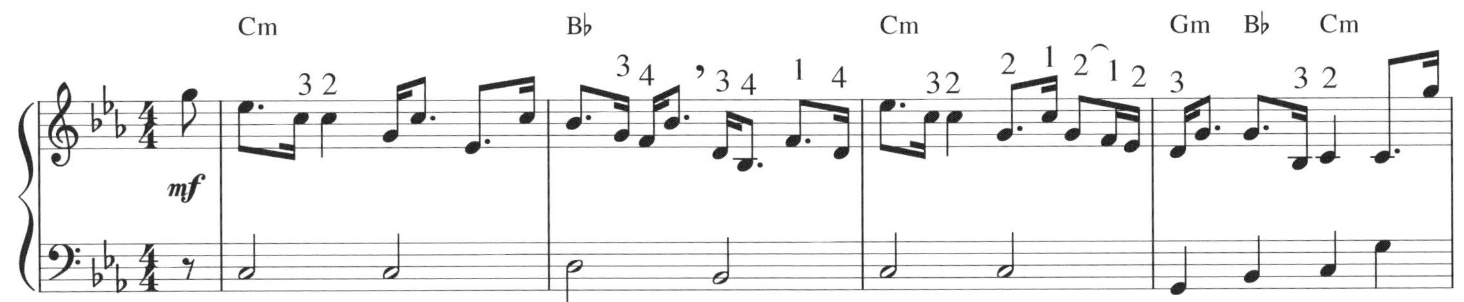

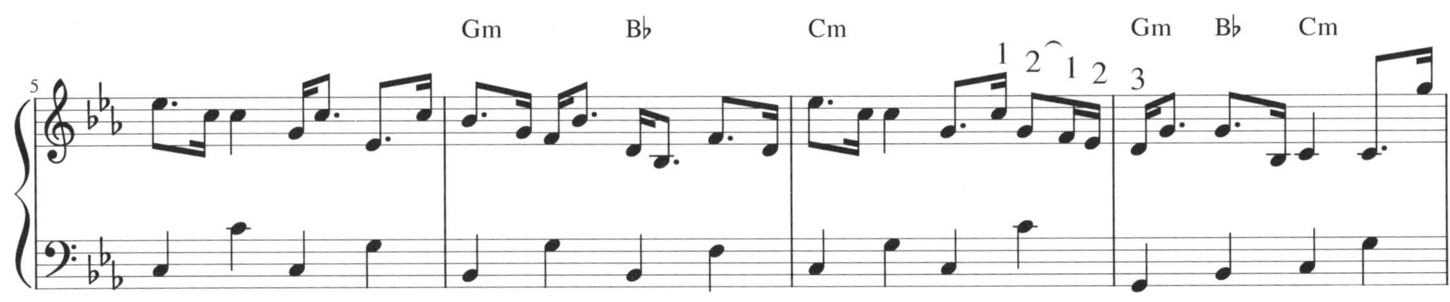

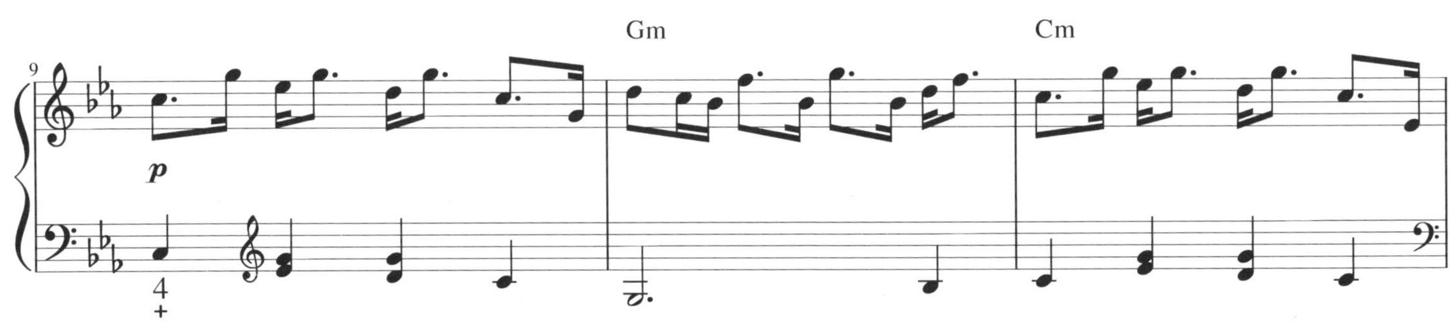

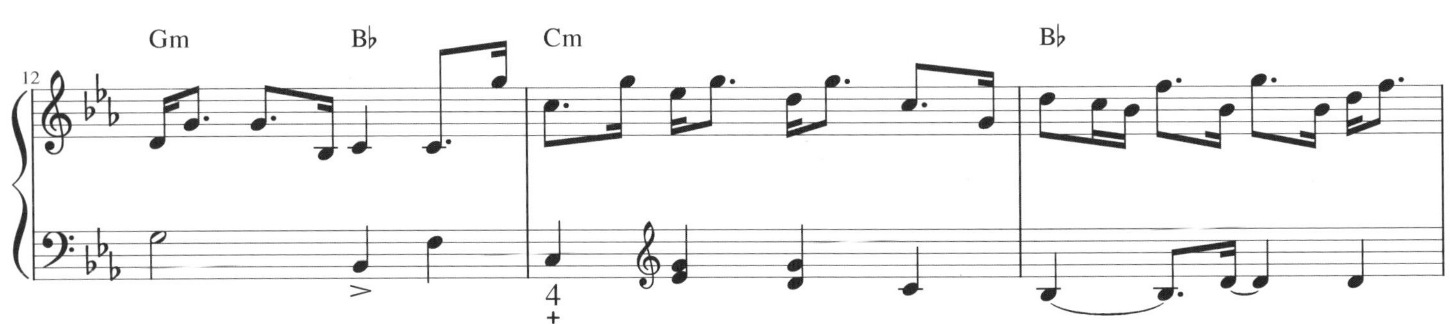

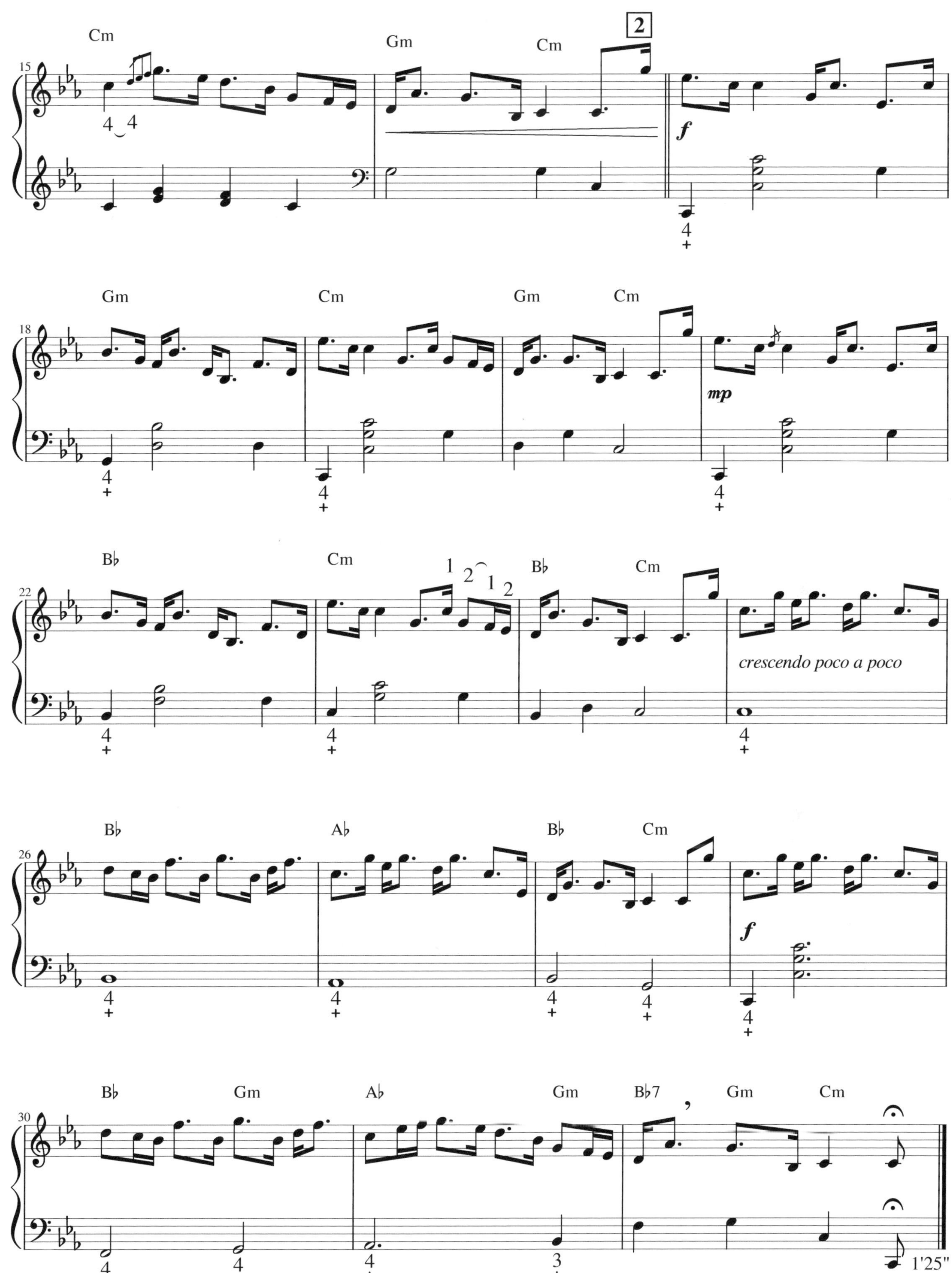
Cm
Gm
Cm
2
f
Gm
Cm
Gm
Cm
mp
B♭
Cm
B♭
Cm
crescendo poco a poco
B♭
A♭
B♭
Cm
f
B♭
Gm
A♭
Gm
B♭7
Gm
Cm
1'25"

The Feet Washing

Reel, Traditional Scottish
Arranged by Stephanie Claussen

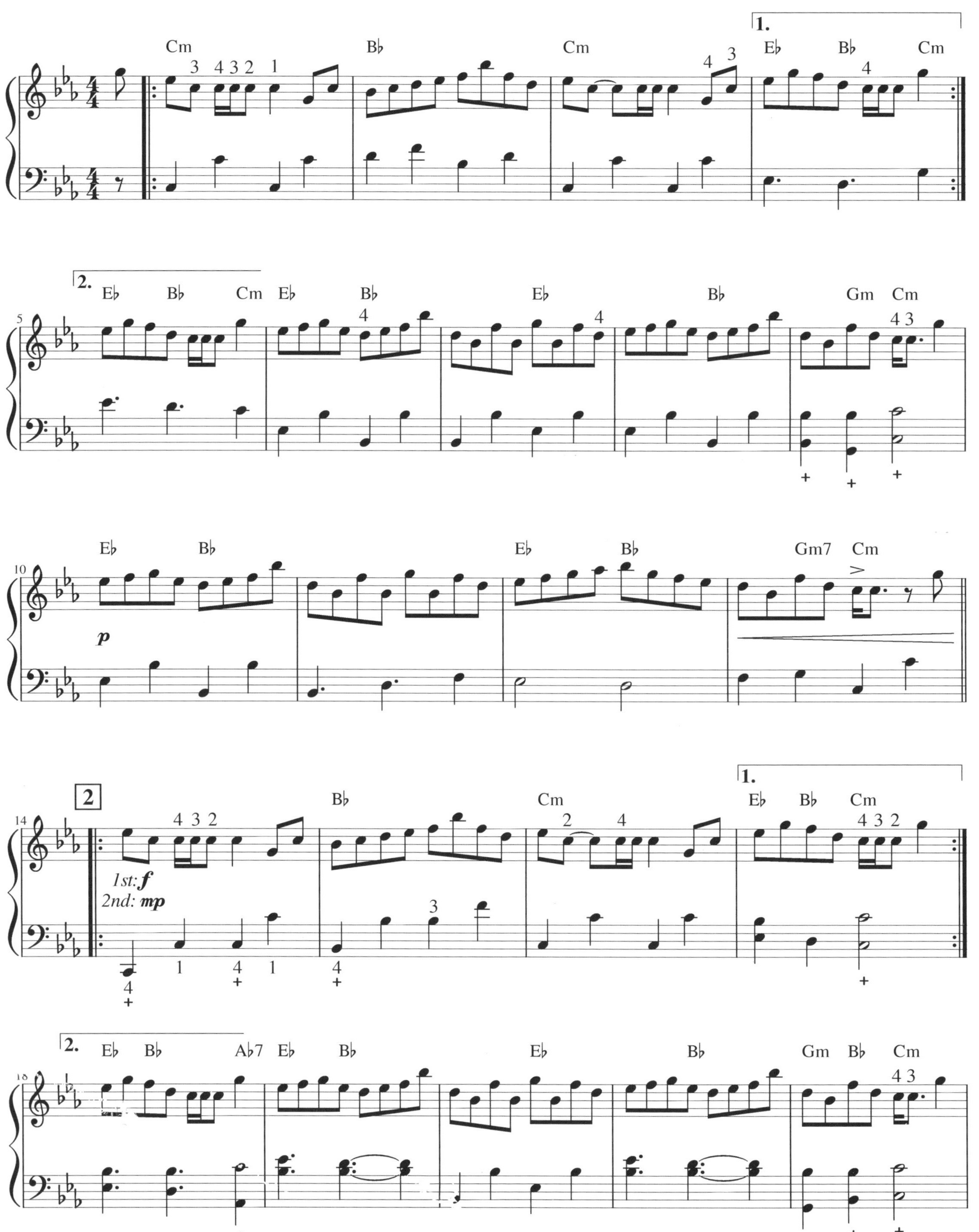

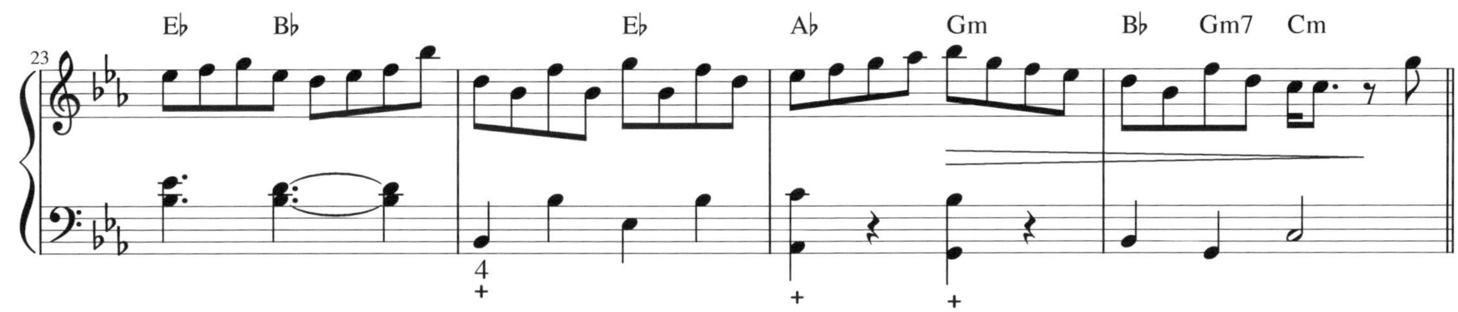

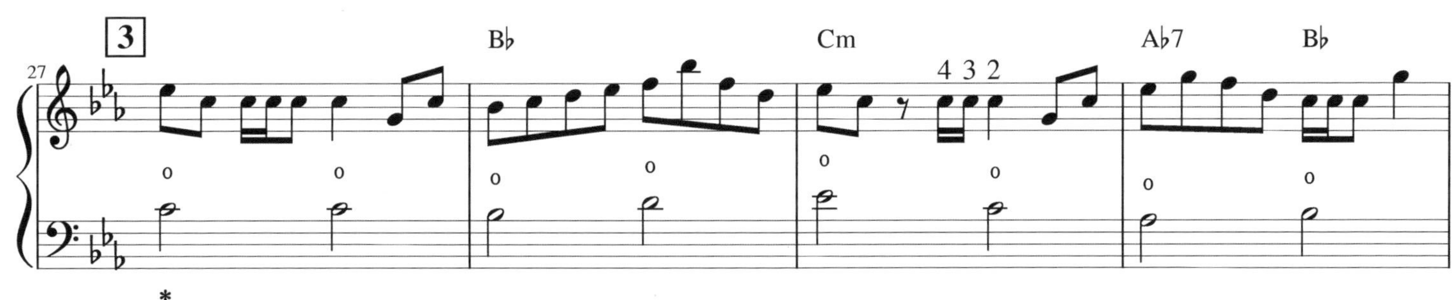

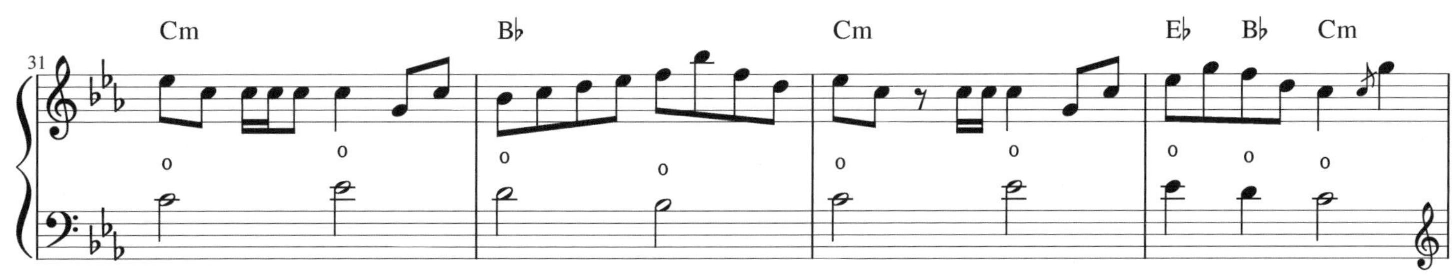

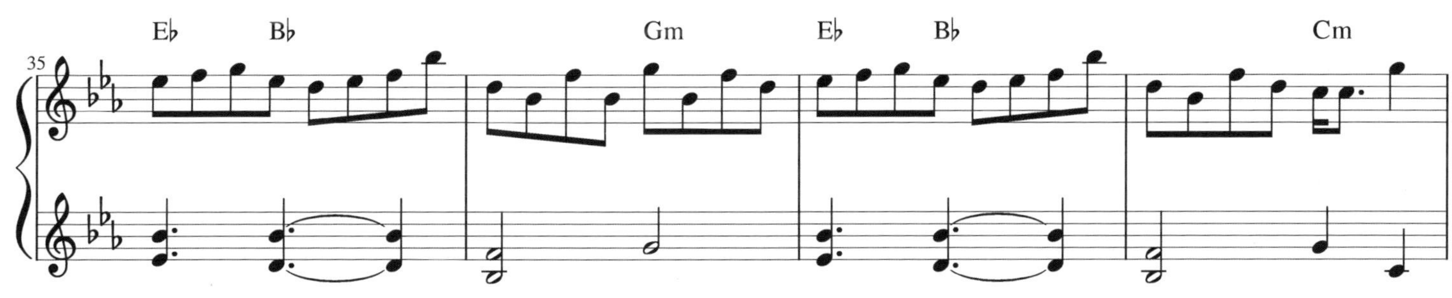

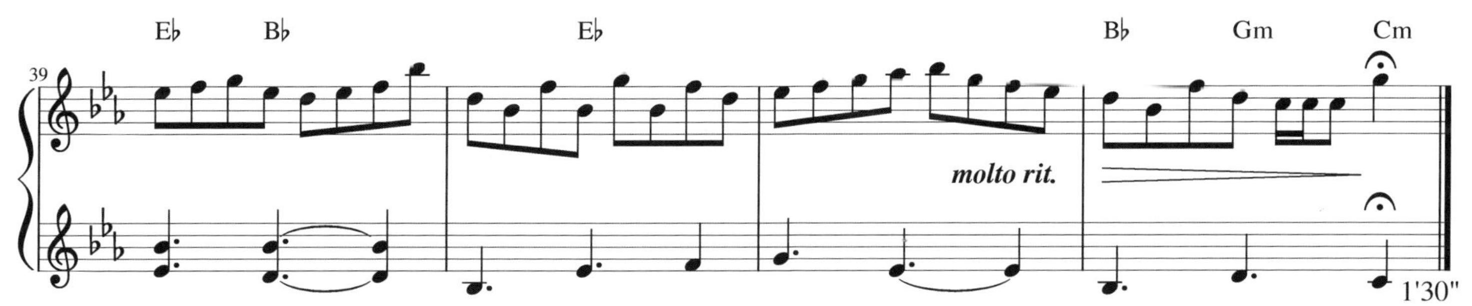

* The harmonics are optional.

The Cold Nights of Winter

Very crisp, magical
Set 2 low F♮s.

Reel, Traditional Shetland
Arranged by Stephanie Claussen

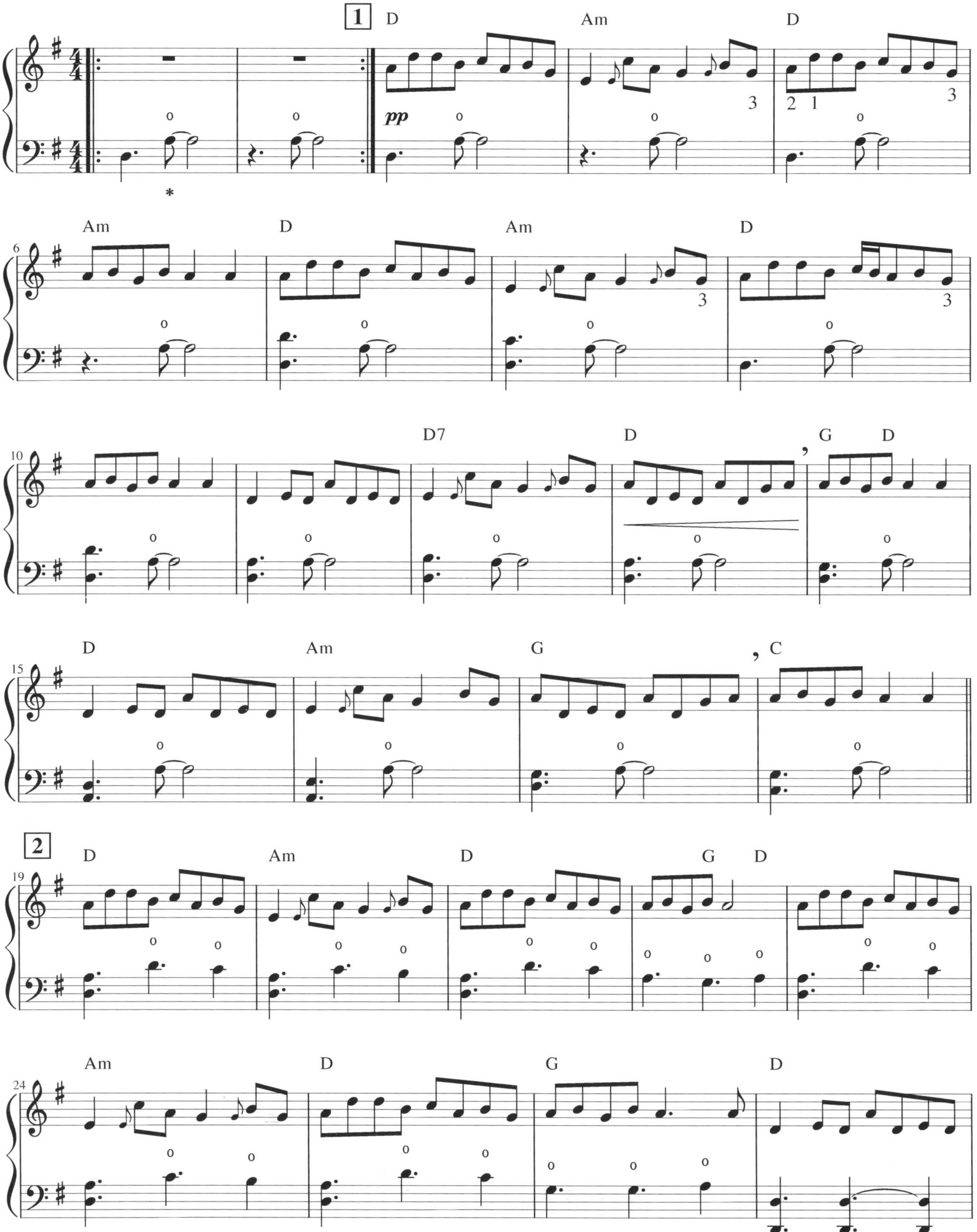

1 D Am D
pp
3 2 1 3

6 Am D Am D
3 3

10 D7 D G D

15 D Am G C

2 D Am D G D
19

24 Am D G D

* The harmonics are optional.

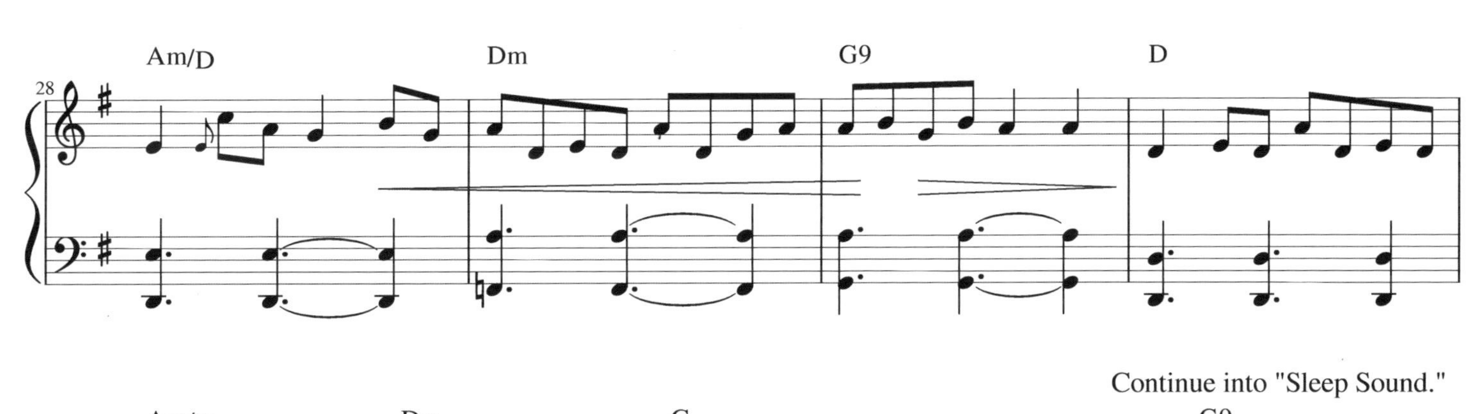

Continue into "Sleep Sound."

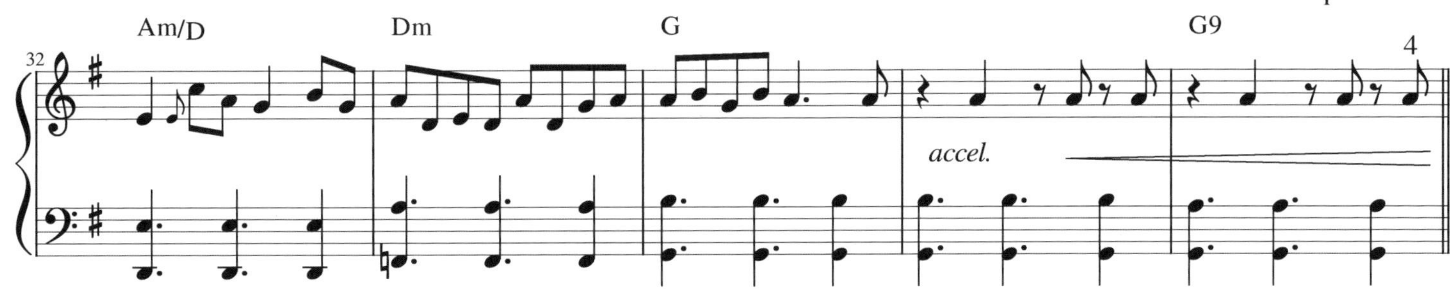

Sleep Sound in the Morning

Furious

Set 2 low F♮s.

Reel, Traditional Shetland

Arranged by Stephanie Claussen

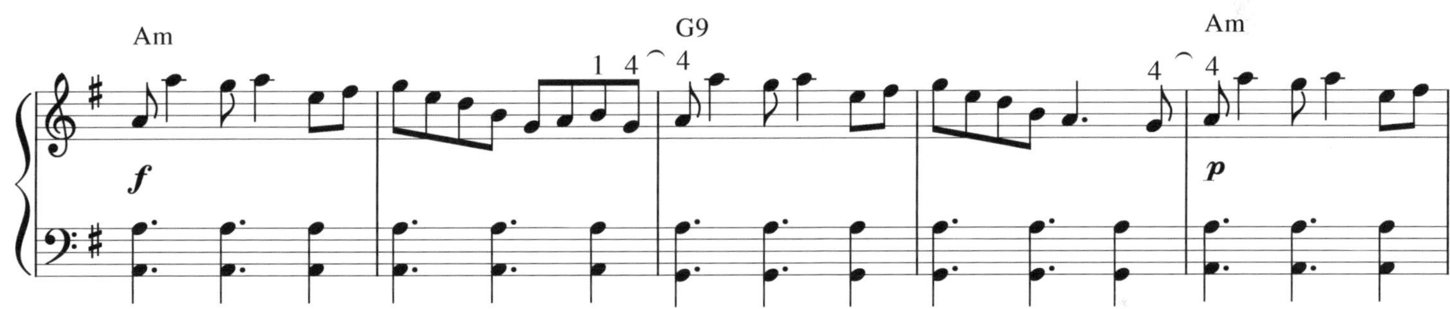

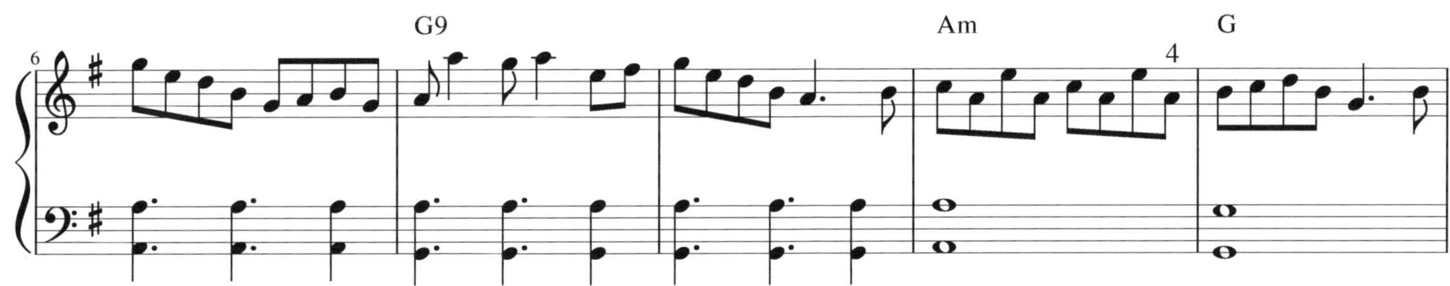

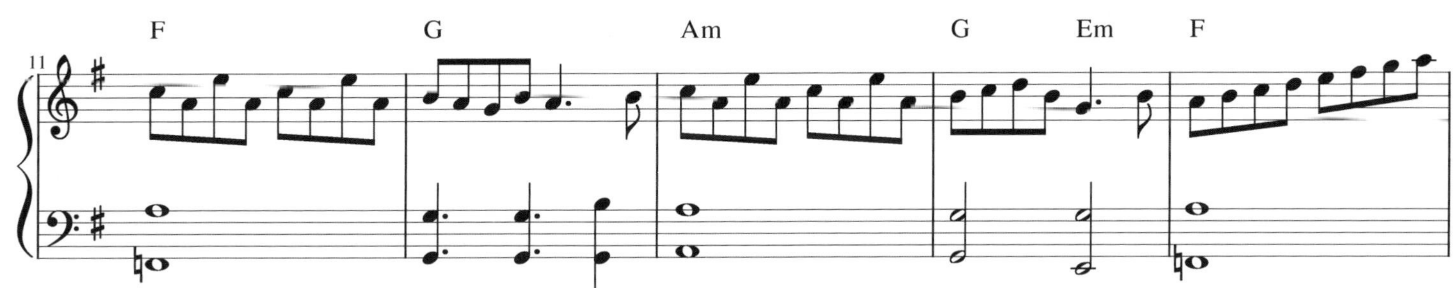

All left-hand octaves, 9ths and 10ths should be played flat.

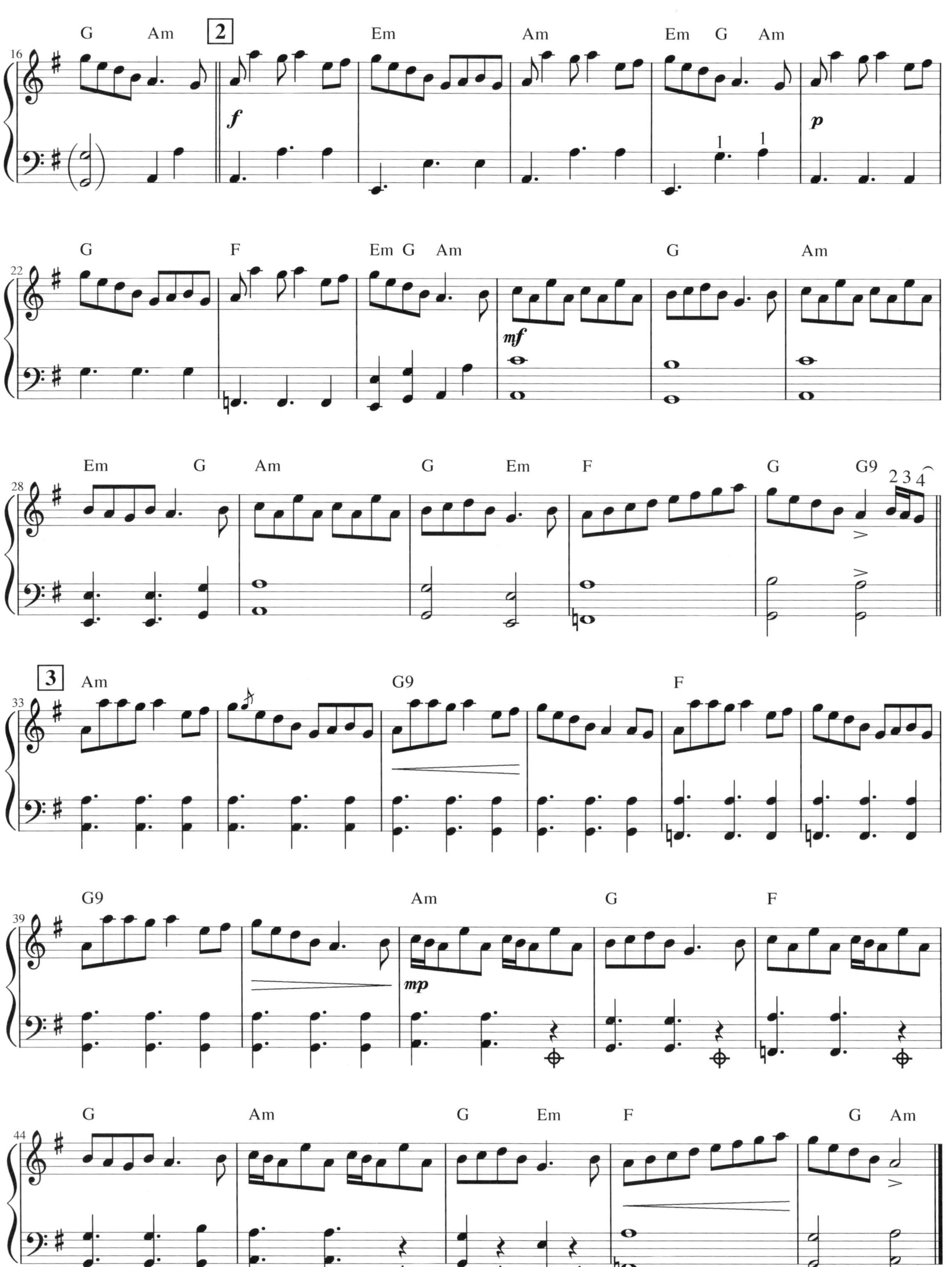

G Am 2 Em Am Em G Am
f
p
G F Em G Am G Am
mf
Em G Am G Em F G G9
3 Am G9 F
G9 Am G F
mp
G Am G Em F G Am
2'58"

The Old Favorite

Jig, Traditional Irish
Arranged by Stephanie Claussen

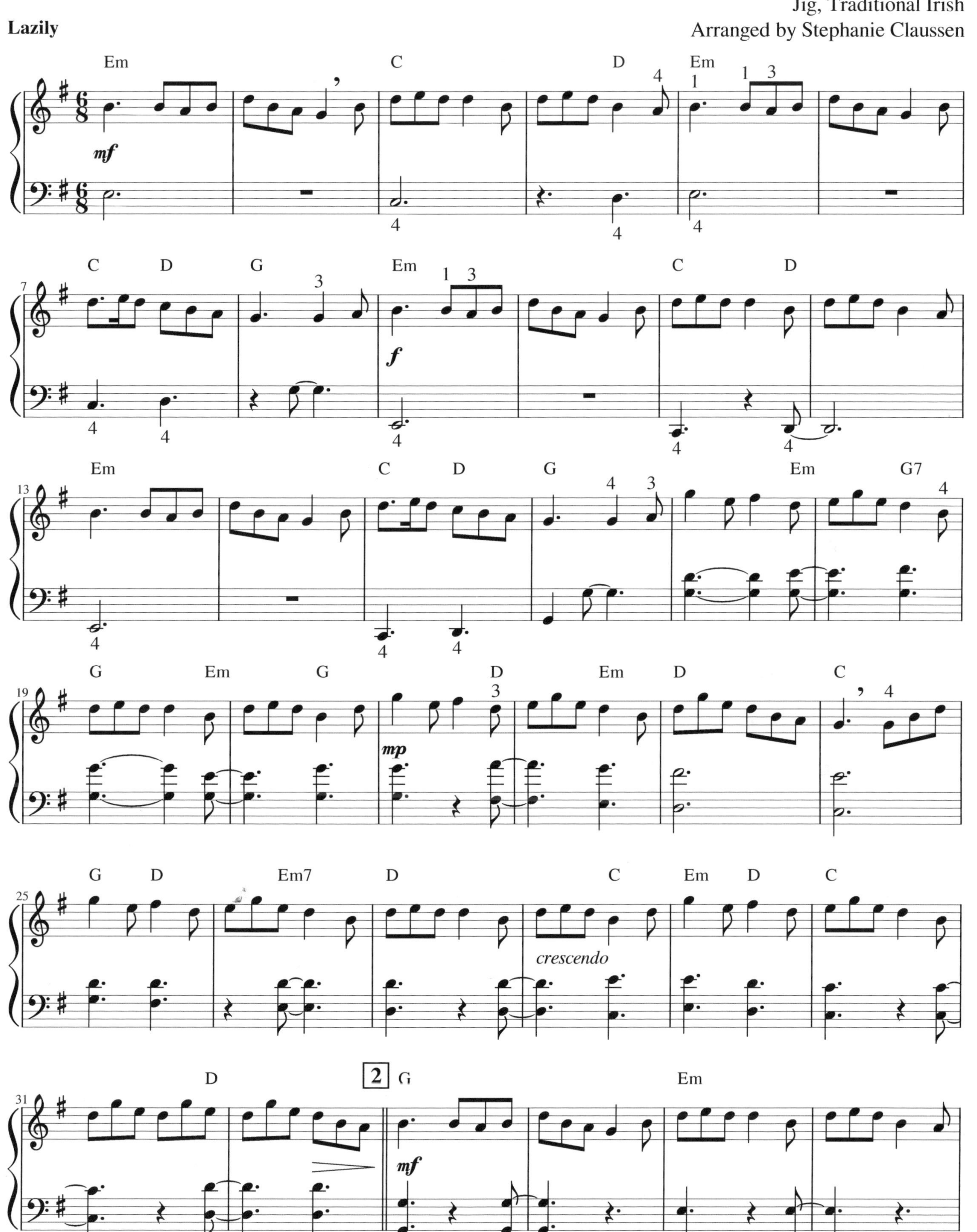

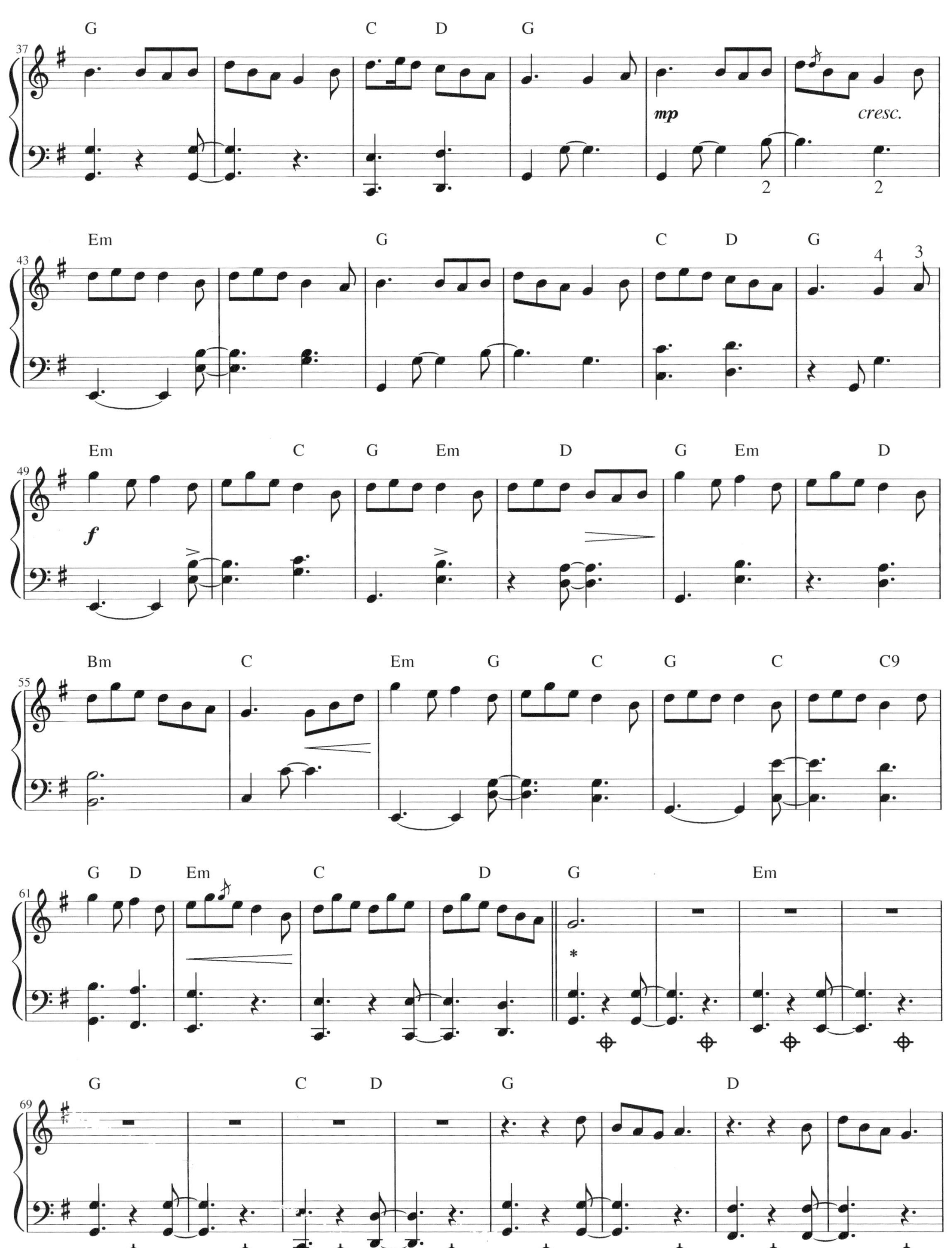

* Replace/muffle as percussively as possible.

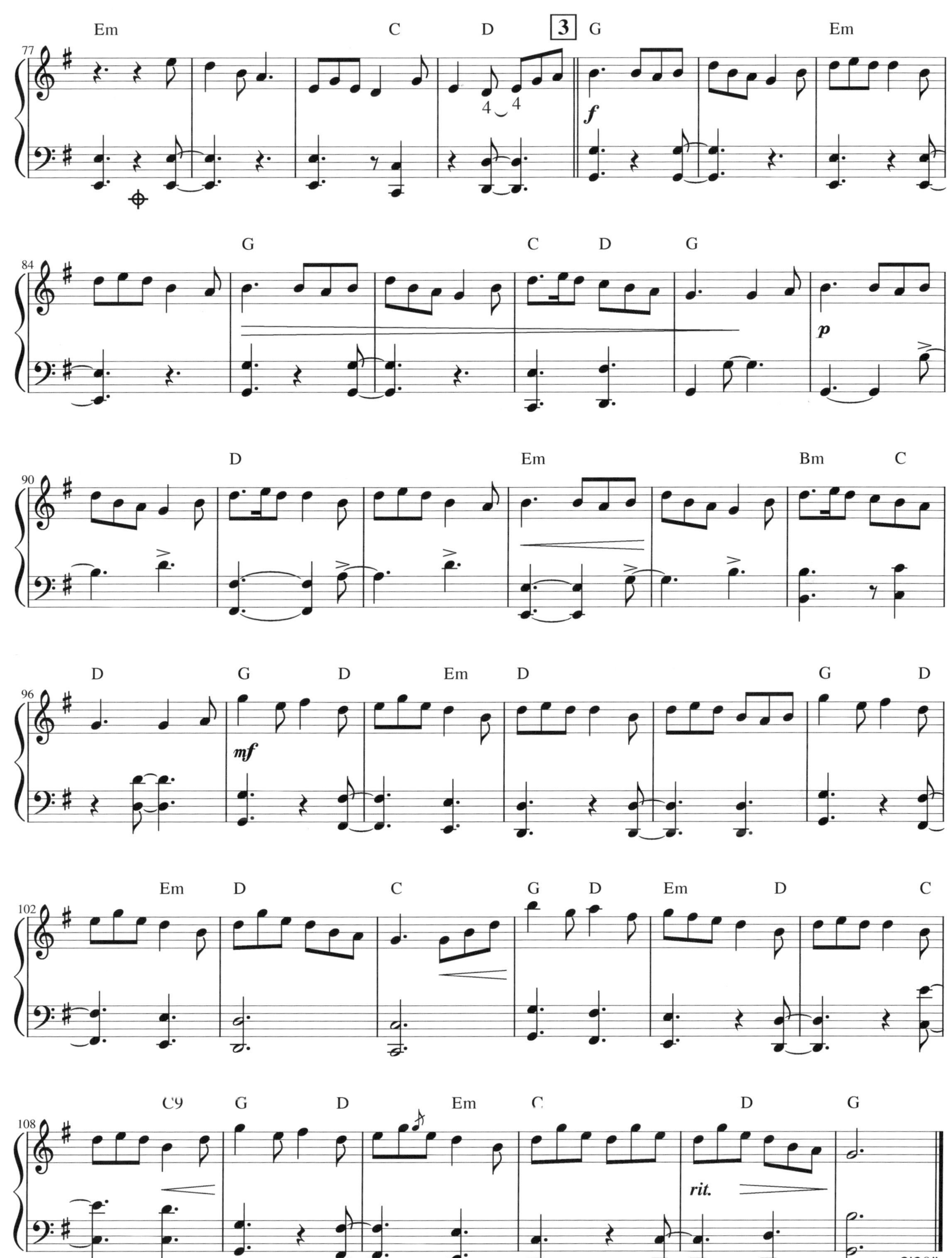

Em C D 3 G Em
f
G C D G
p
D Em Bm C
D G D Em D G D
mf
Em D C G D Em D C
C9 G D Em C D G
rit.
2'20"

This Gloom On My Soul

Air, Traditional Scottish
Arranged by Stephanie Claussen

Achingly slow and sweet

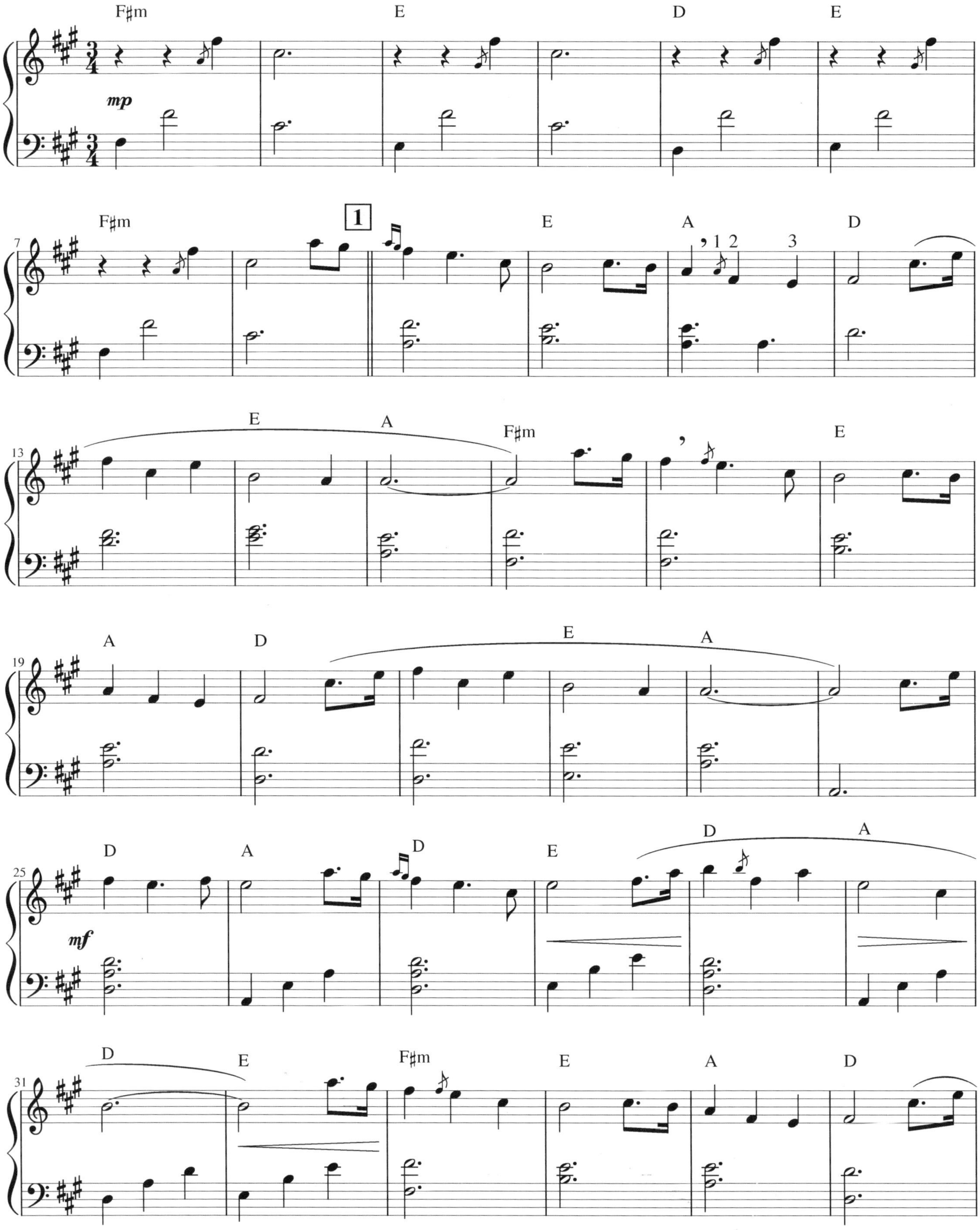

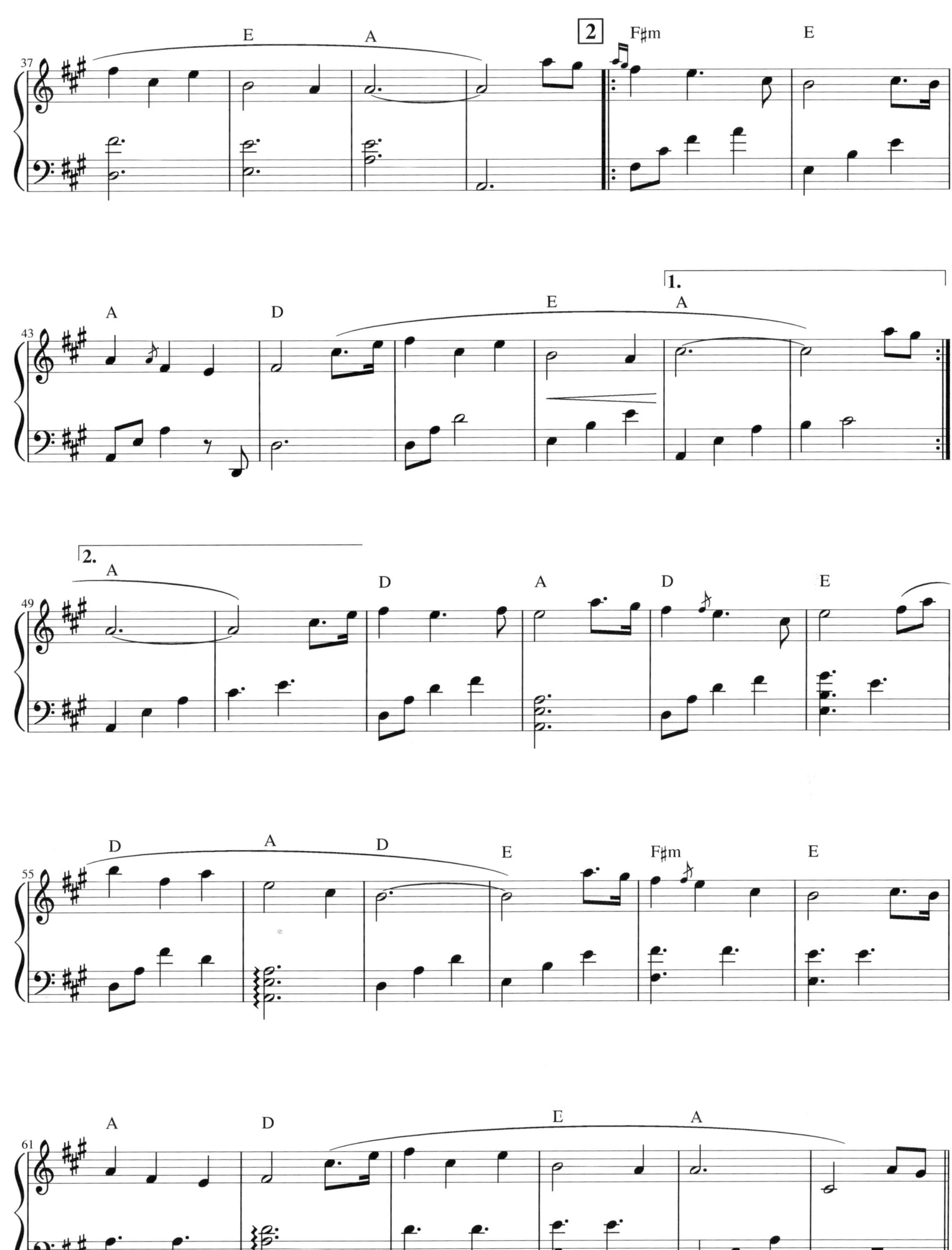
37
E
A
2
F♯m
E
43
A
D
E
1.
A
49
2.
A
D
A
D
E
55
D
A
D
E
F♯m
E
61
A
D
E
A

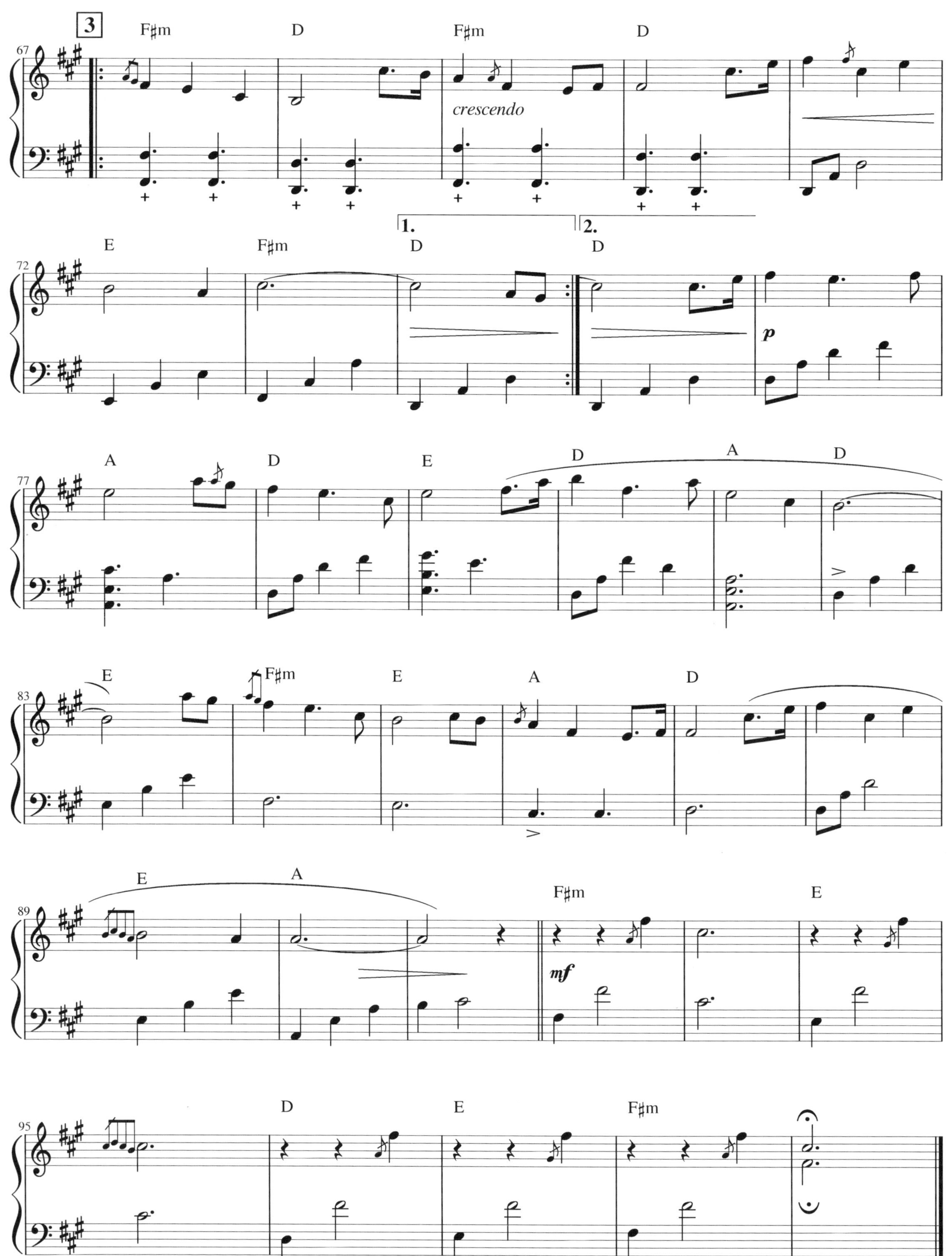
3
F♯m
D
F♯m
D
crescendo
1.
2.
E
F♯m
D
D
p
A
D
E
D
A
D
E
F♯m
E
A
D
E
A
F♯m
E
mf
D
E
F♯m
3'55"

Planxty Drew

by Turlough O'Carolan
Arranged by Stephanie Claussen

Impish

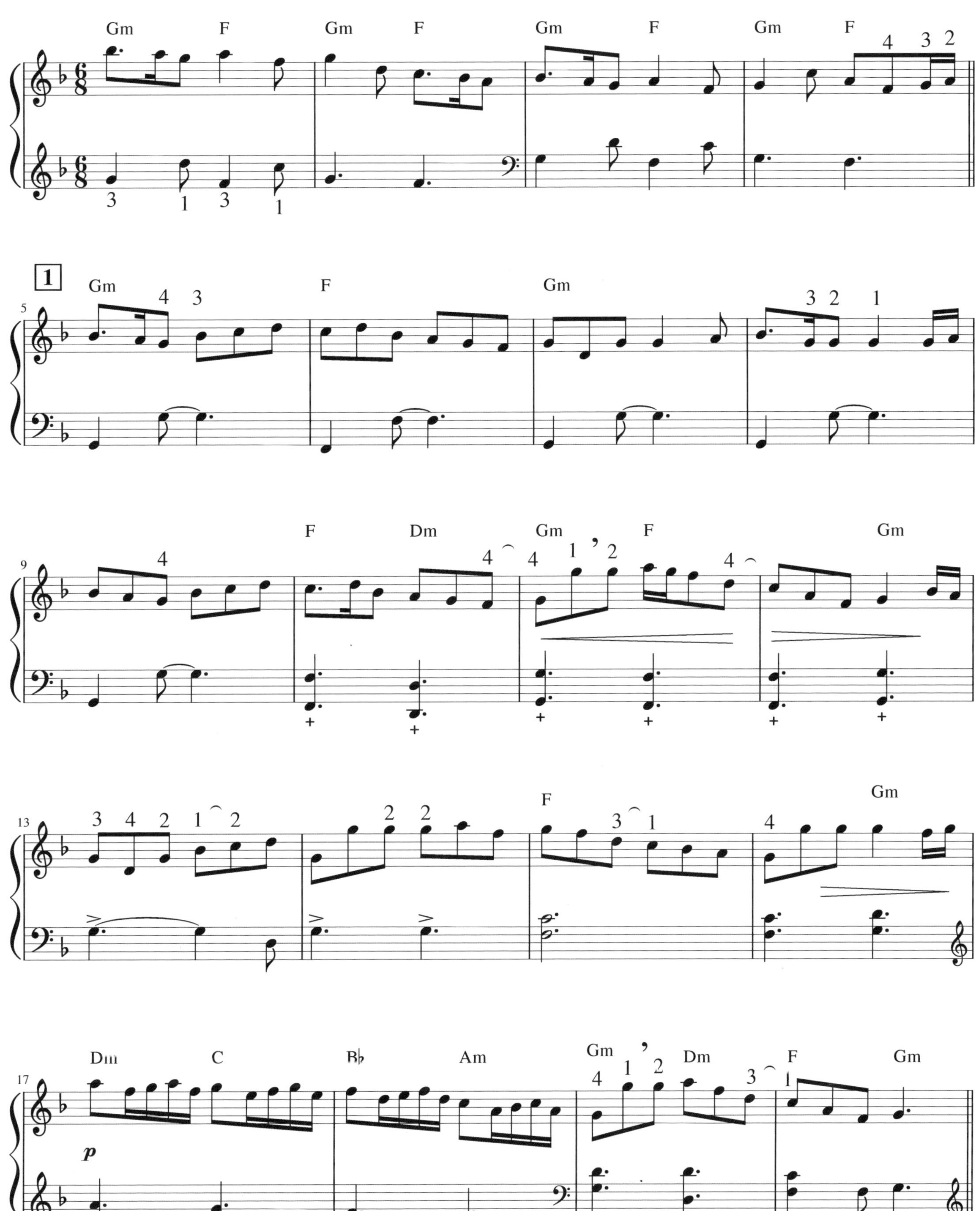

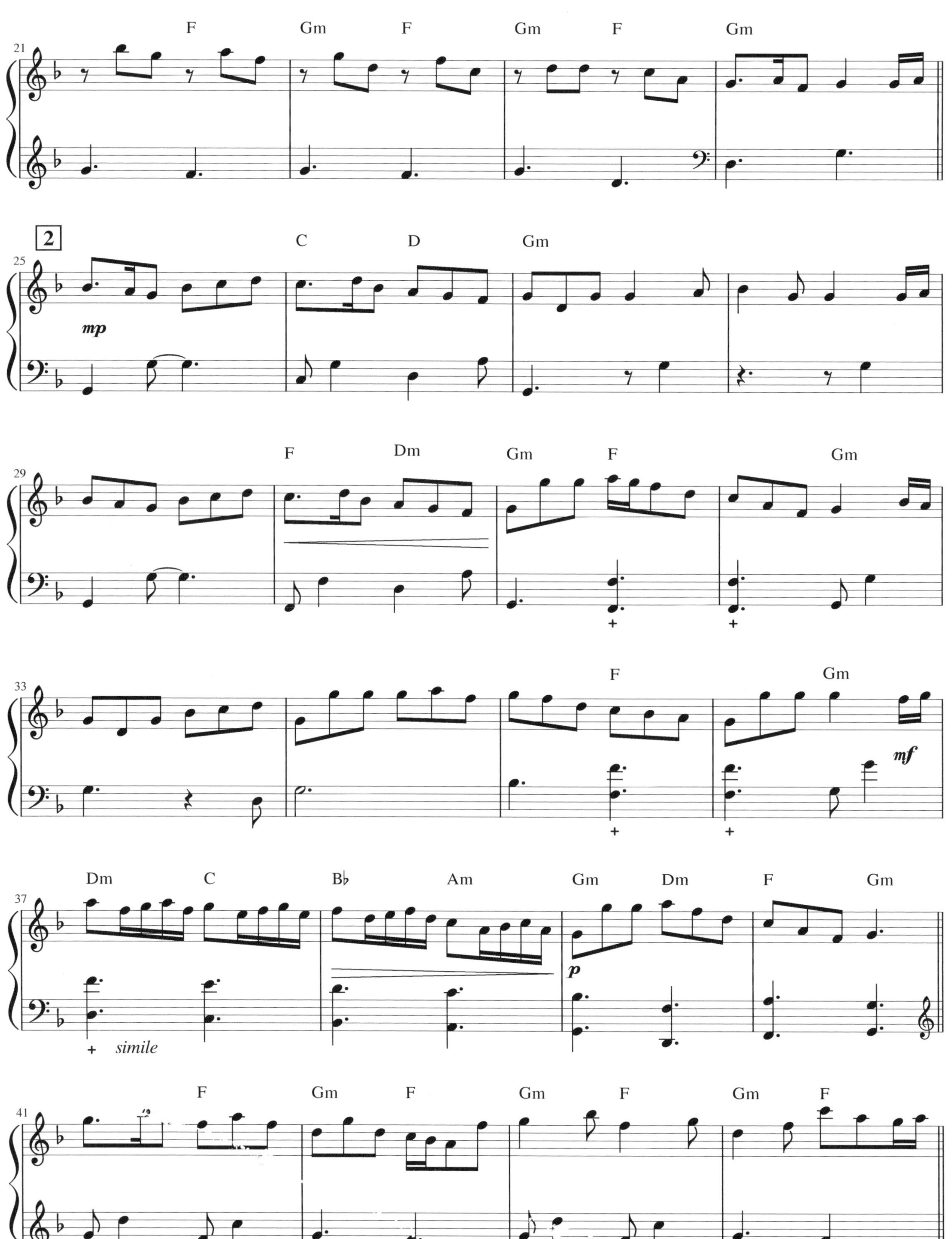
F
Gm
F
Gm
F
Gm
2
C
D
Gm
mp
F
Dm
Gm
F
Gm
F
Gm
mf
Dm
C
B♭
Am
Gm
Dm
F
Gm
simile
p
F
Gm
F
Gm
F
Gm
F

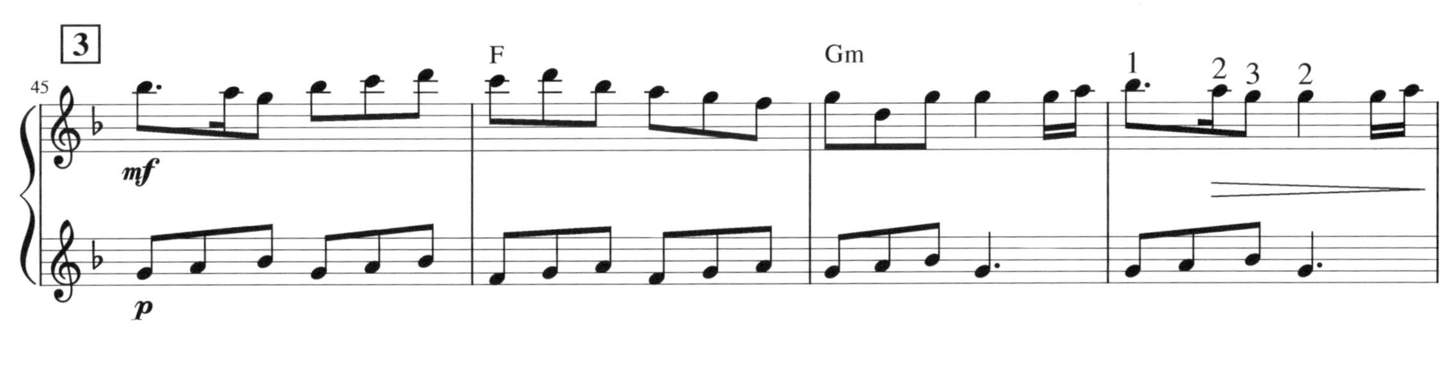

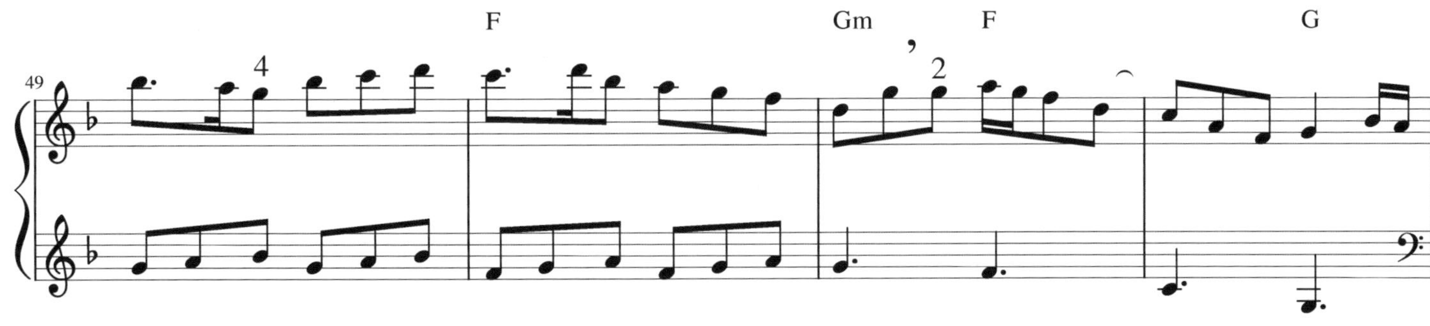

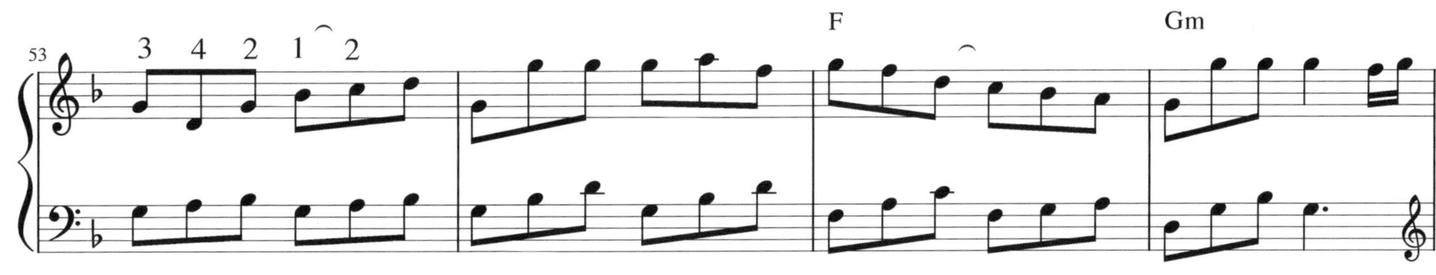

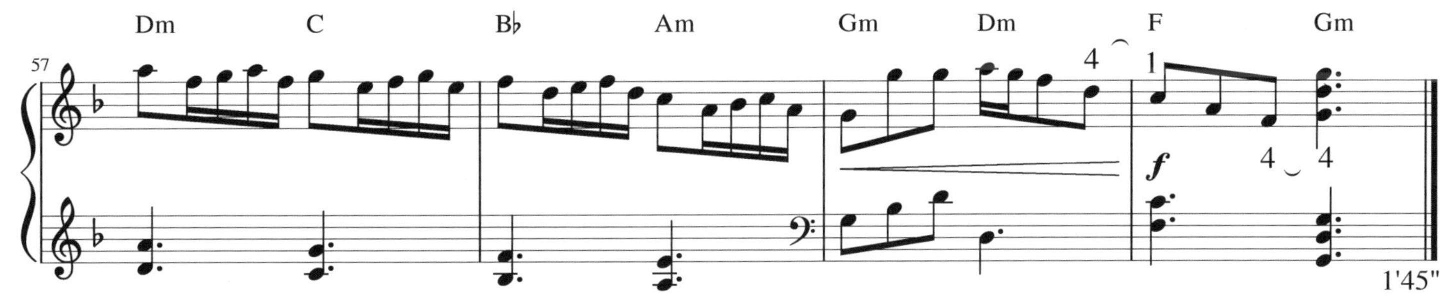

Transition into "Miss Noble"

(If continuing into "Miss Noble," play the transition instead of the final chord of "Planxty Drew.")

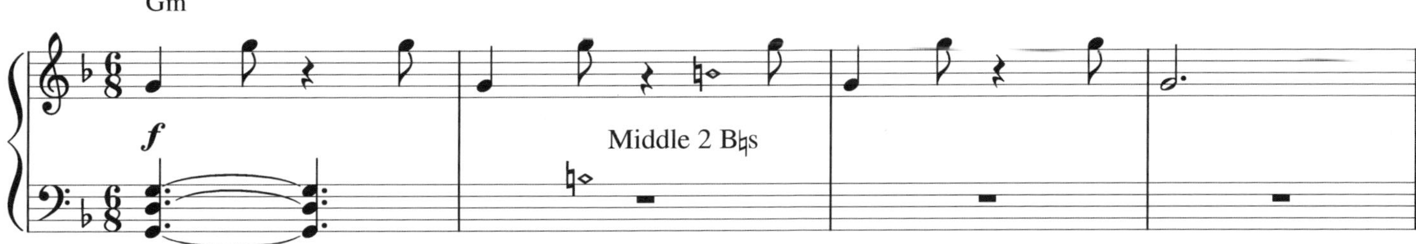

Miss Noble

by Turlough O'Carolan
Arranged by Stephanie Claussen

Casual, and a little bit quirky

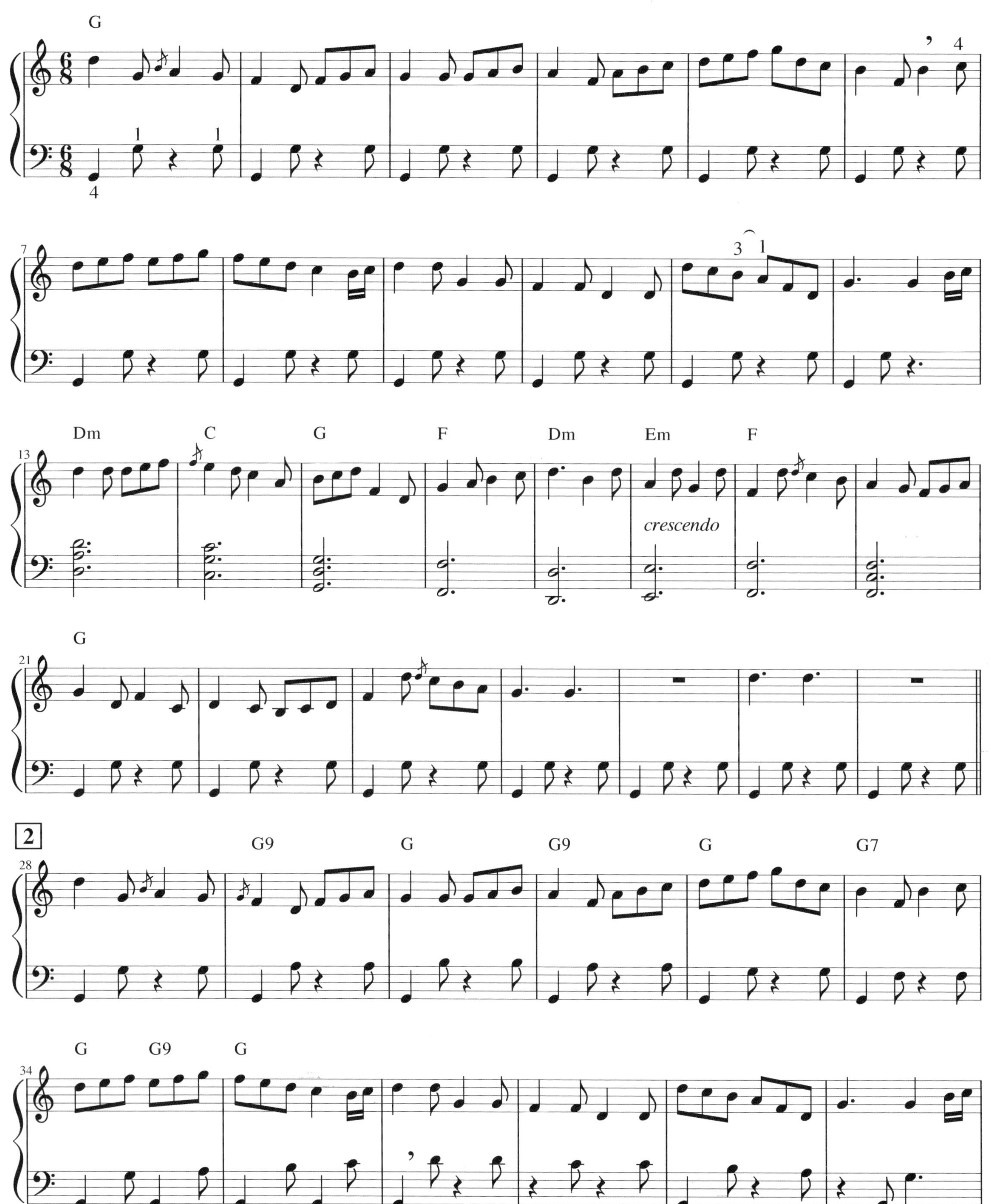

All left-hand octaves, 9ths, and 10ths, broken or otherwise, should be played flat.

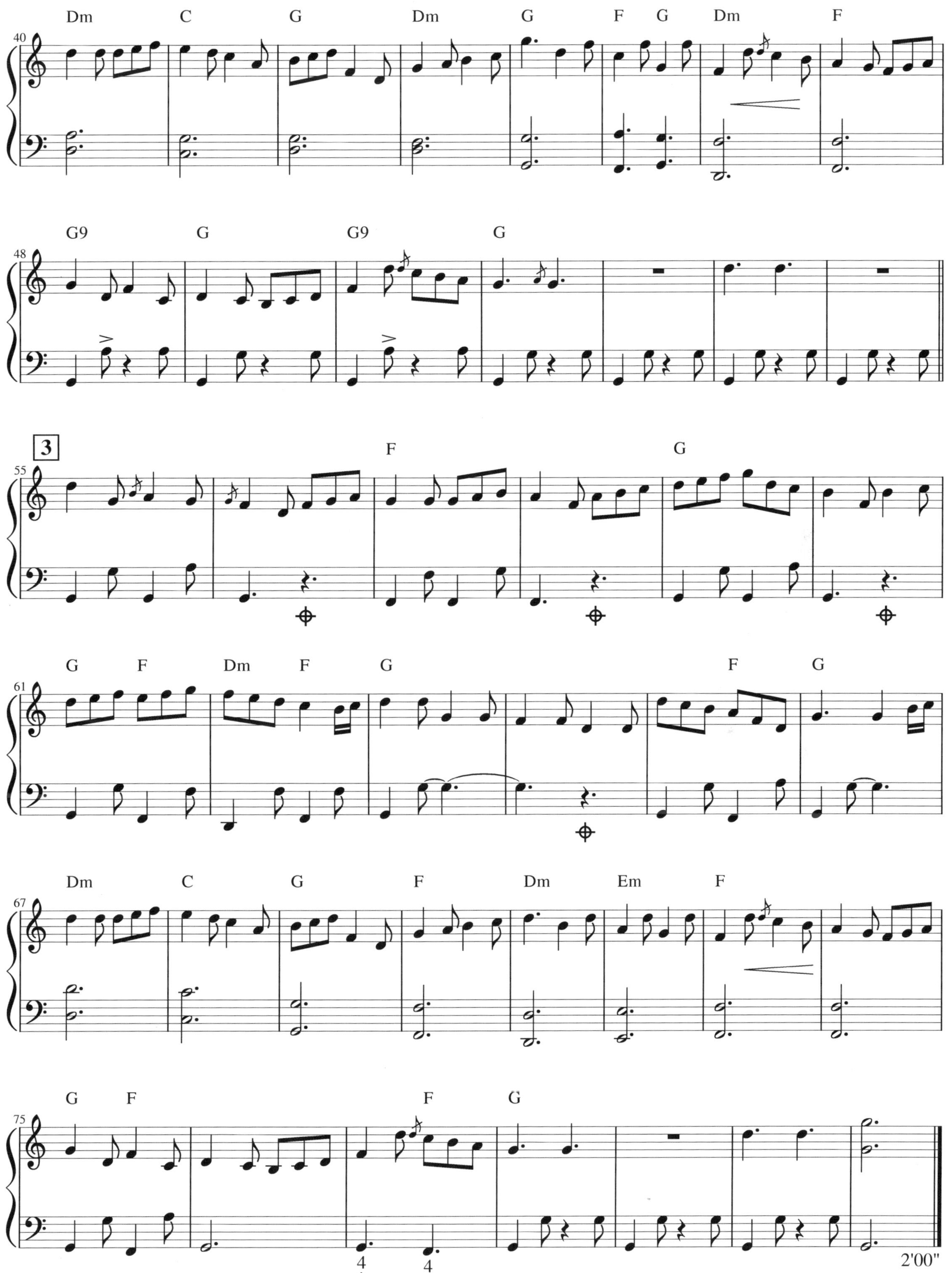
Dm C G Dm G F G Dm F
40
G9 G G9 G
48
3
F G
55
G F Dm F G F G
61
Dm C G F Dm Em F
67
G F F G
75
4
+
4
+
2'00"

The Forest Where the Deer Resort

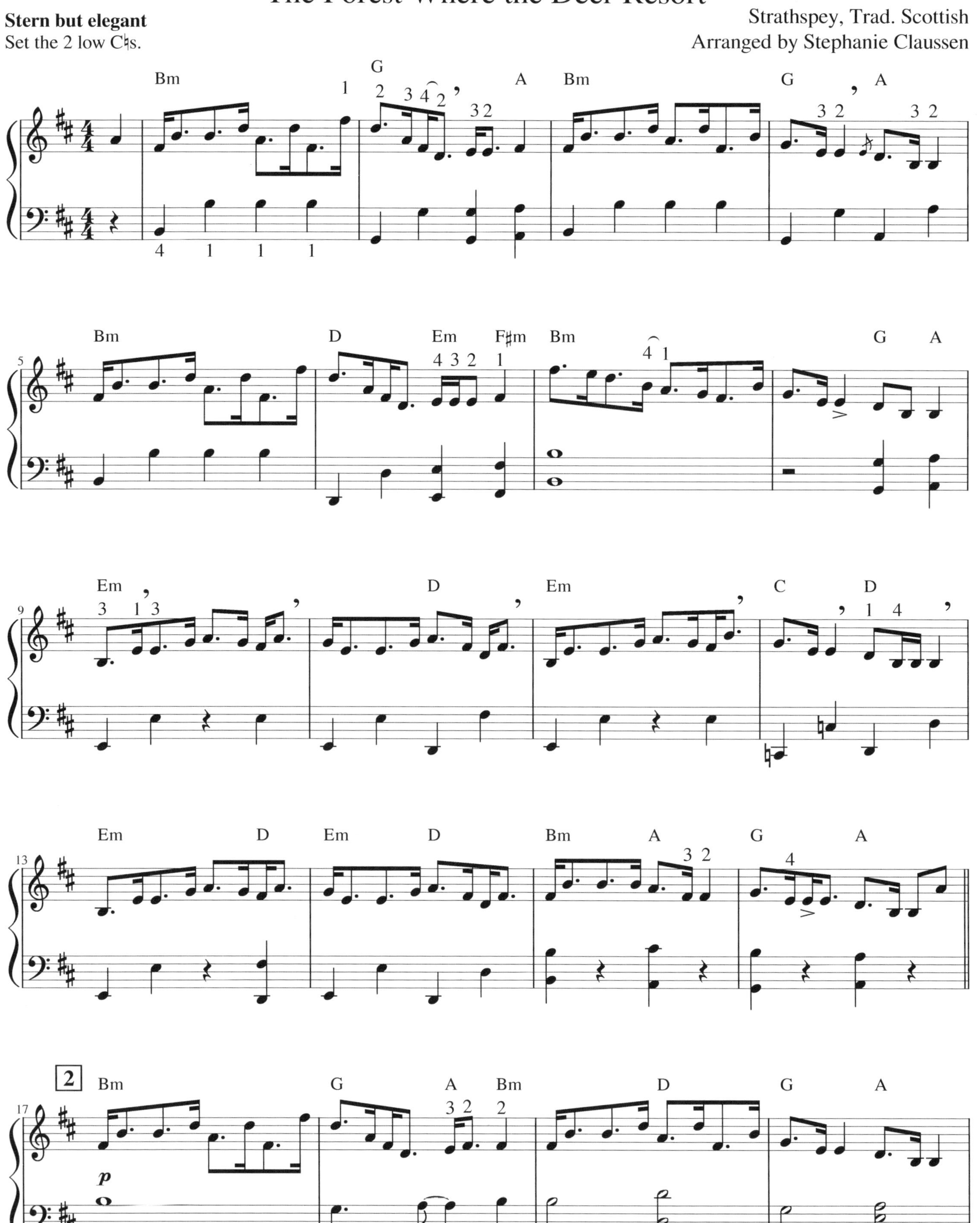

All left-hand octaves, broken or otherwise, should be played flat.

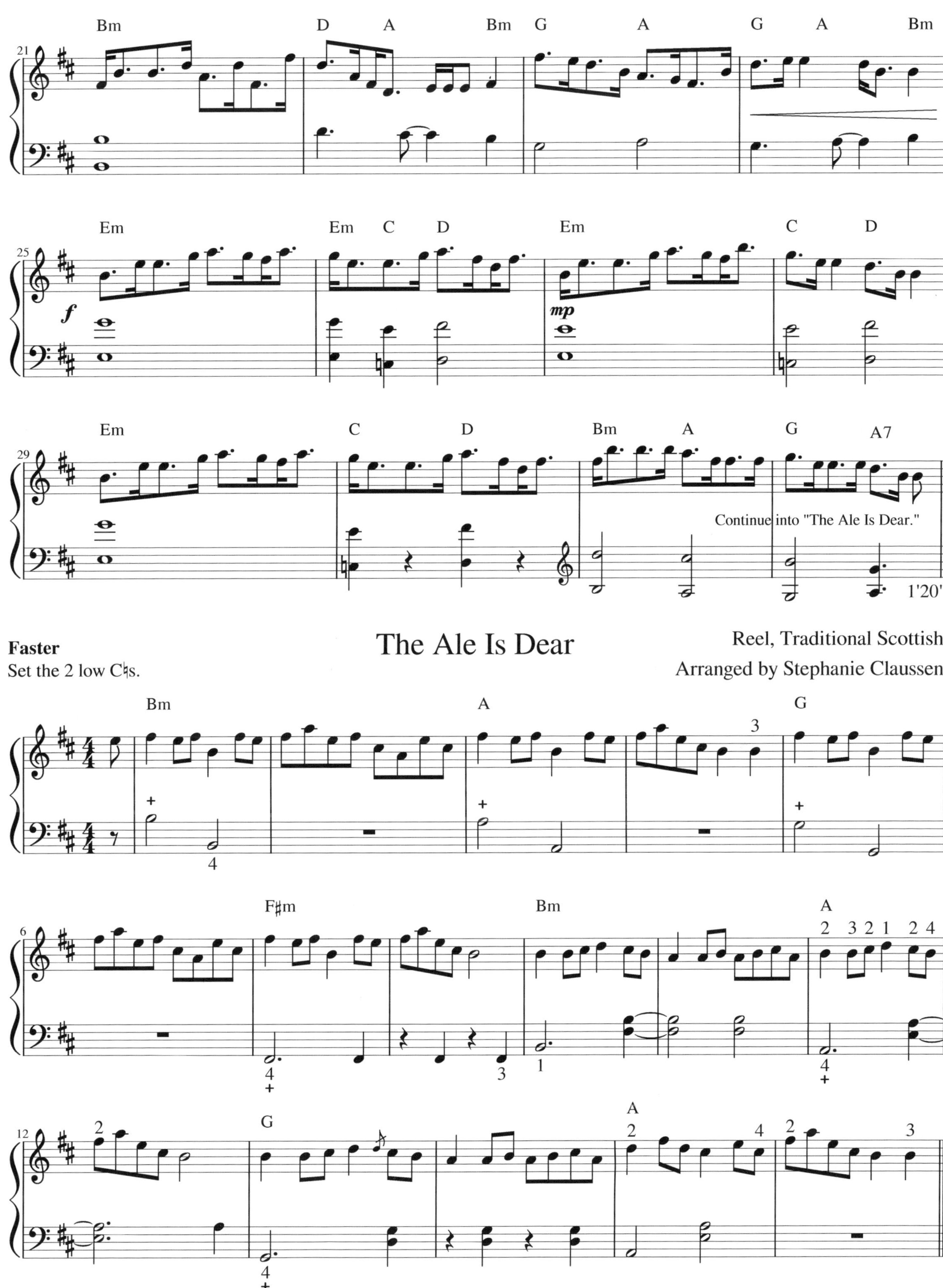
Bm
D A Bm
G A
G A Bm
Em
f
Em C D
Em
mp
C D
Em
C D
Bm A
G A7
Continue into "The Ale Is Dear."
1'20"
Faster
Set the 2 low C♮s.
The Ale Is Dear
Reel, Traditional Scottish
Arranged by Stephanie Claussen
Bm
A
G
F♯m
Bm
A
G
A

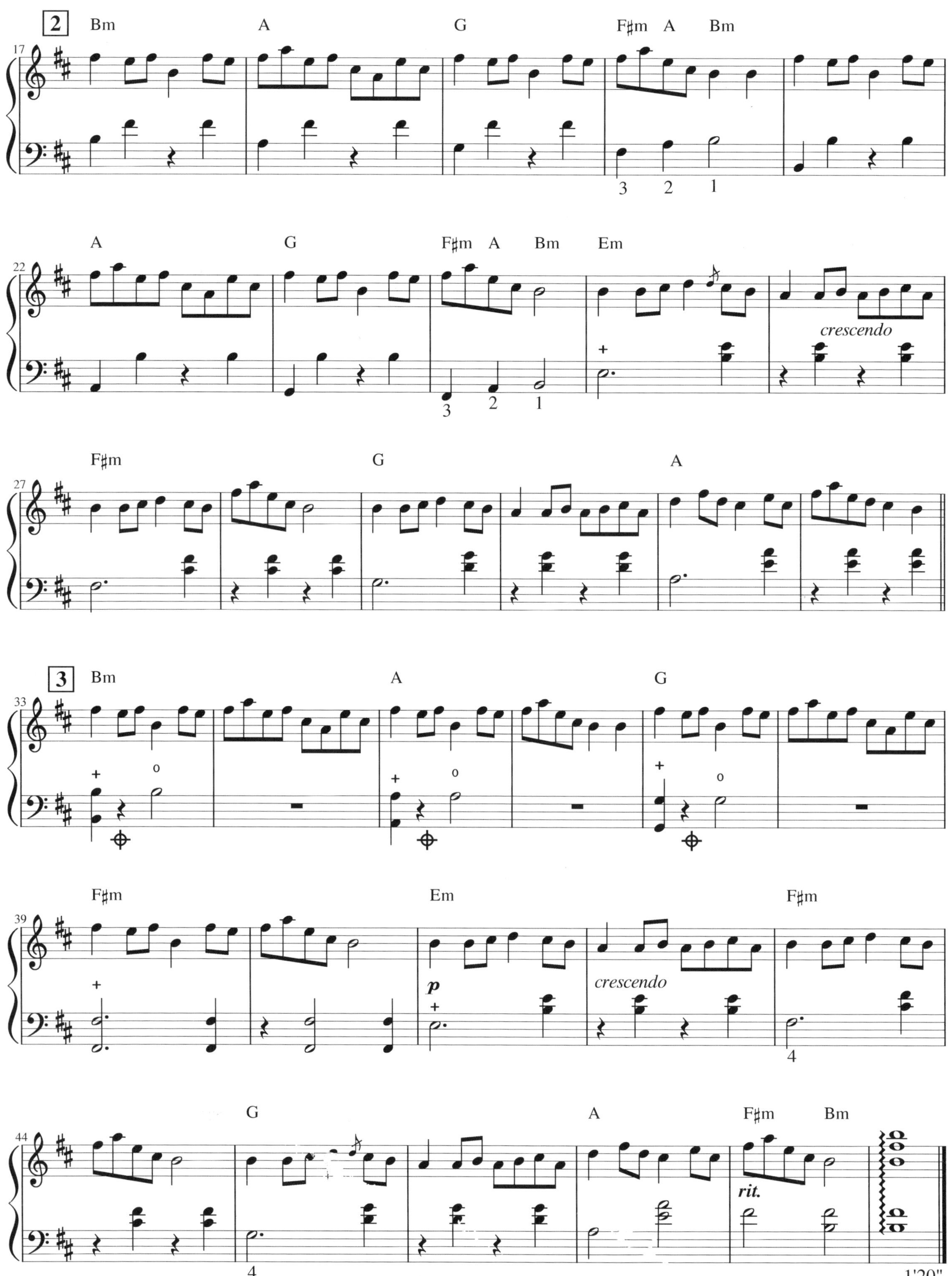
2
Bm
A
G
F♯m A Bm
A
G
F♯m A Bm
Em
crescendo
F♯m
G
A
3
Bm
A
G
F♯m
Em
p
crescendo
F♯m
G
A
F♯m
Bm
rit.
1'20"

Lord Huntley's Cave

by James Scott Skinner
Arranged by Stephanie Claussen

Scottish March

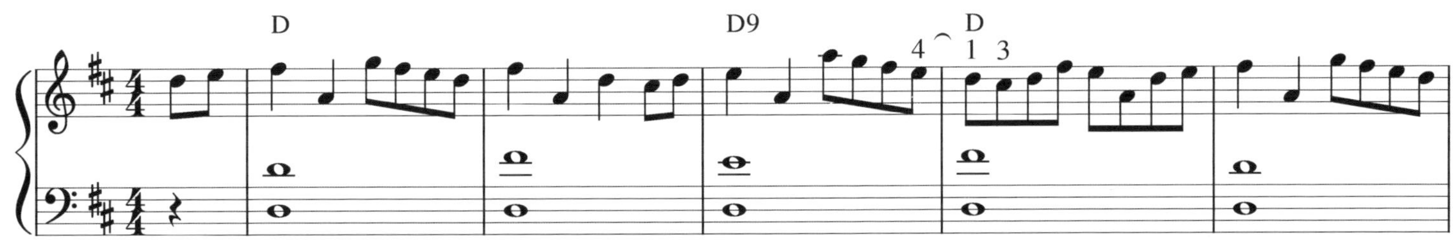

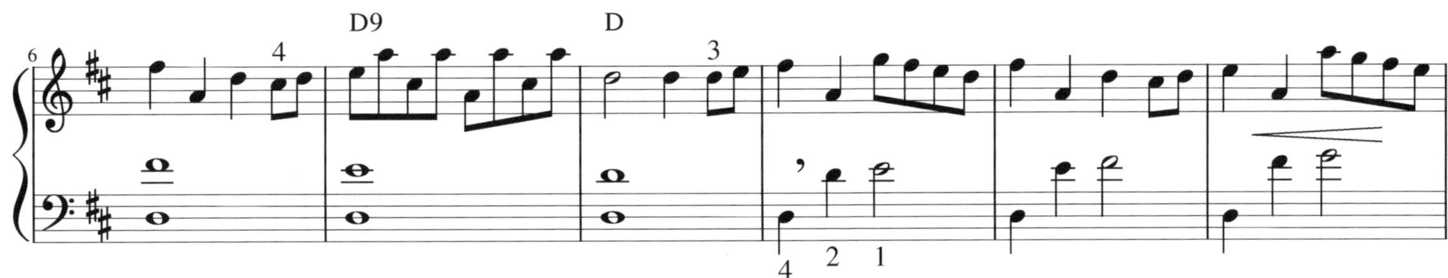

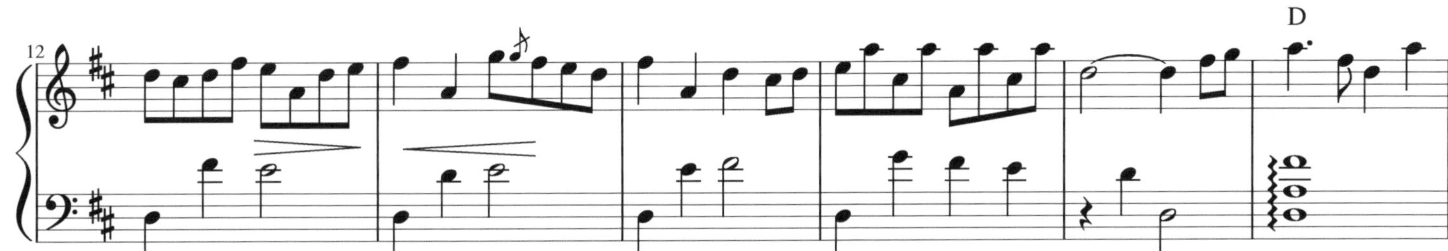

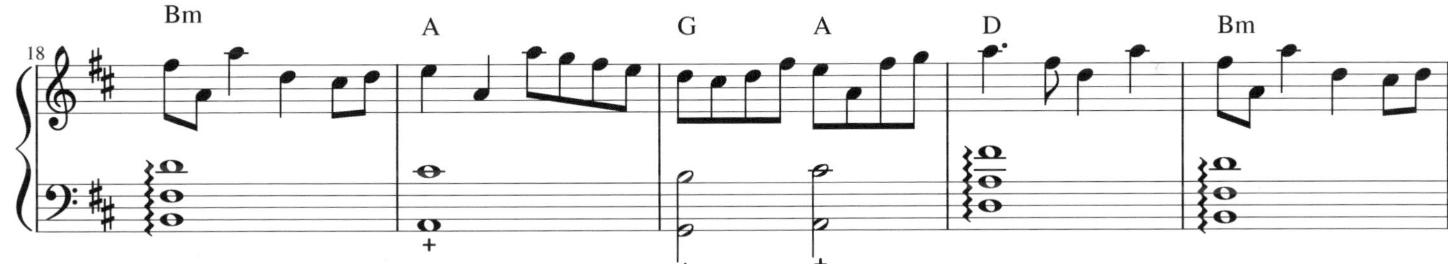

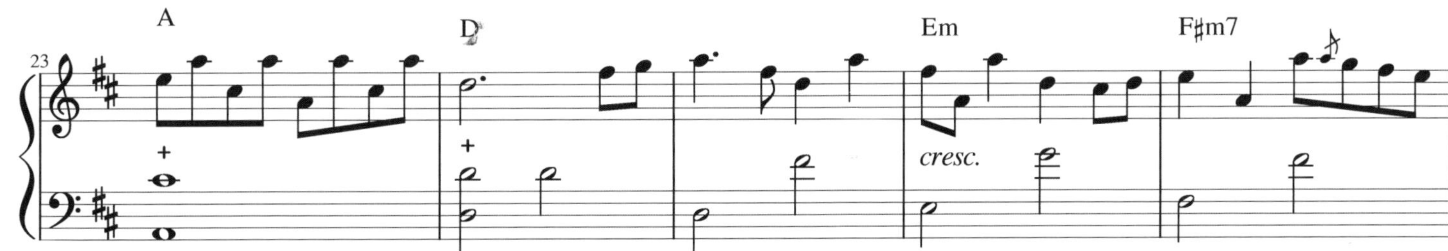

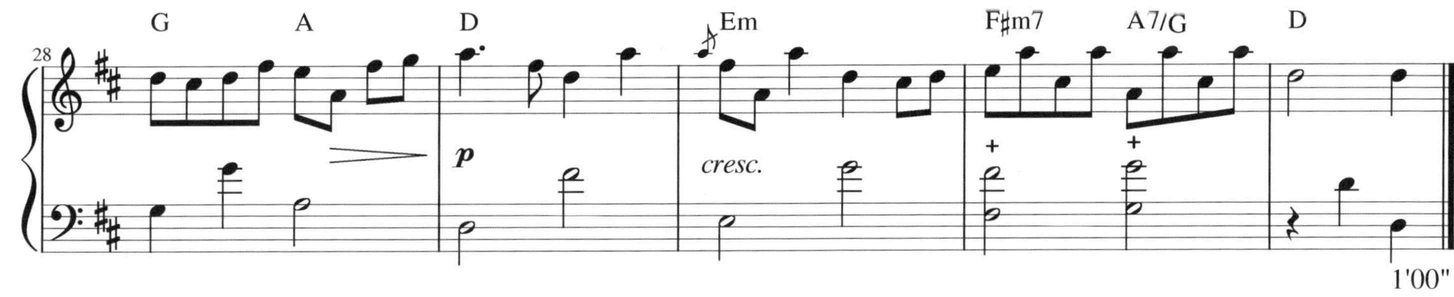

The Parting Glass

Traditional Irish
Arranged by Stephanie Claussen

Rhythmic, but with room to breathe

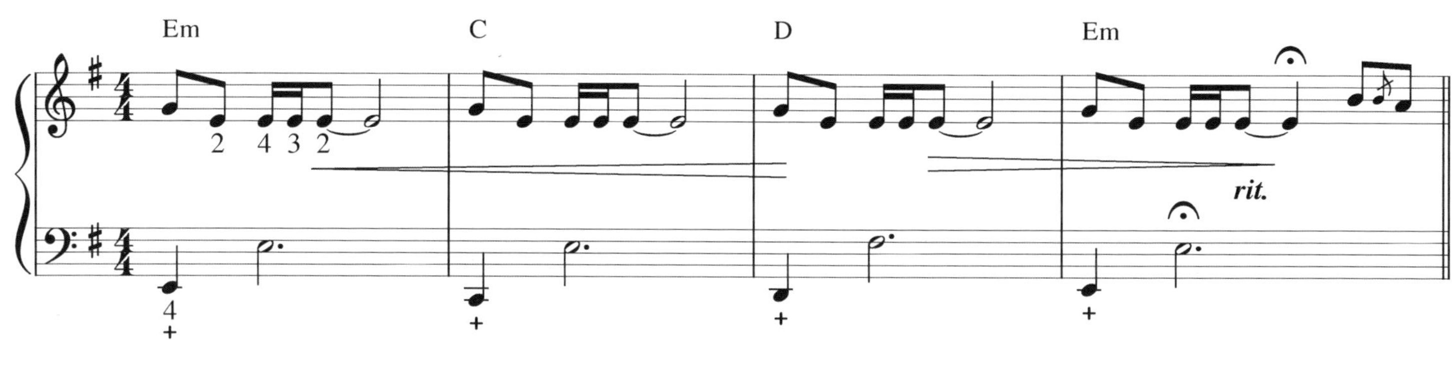

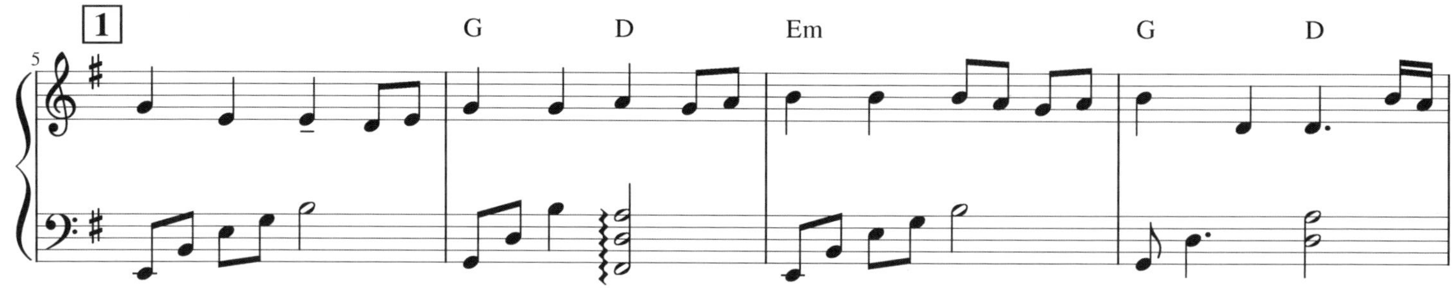

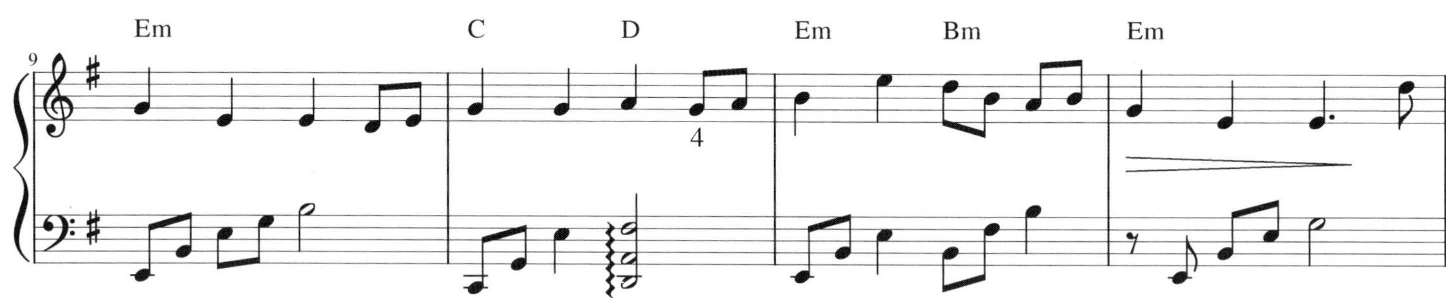

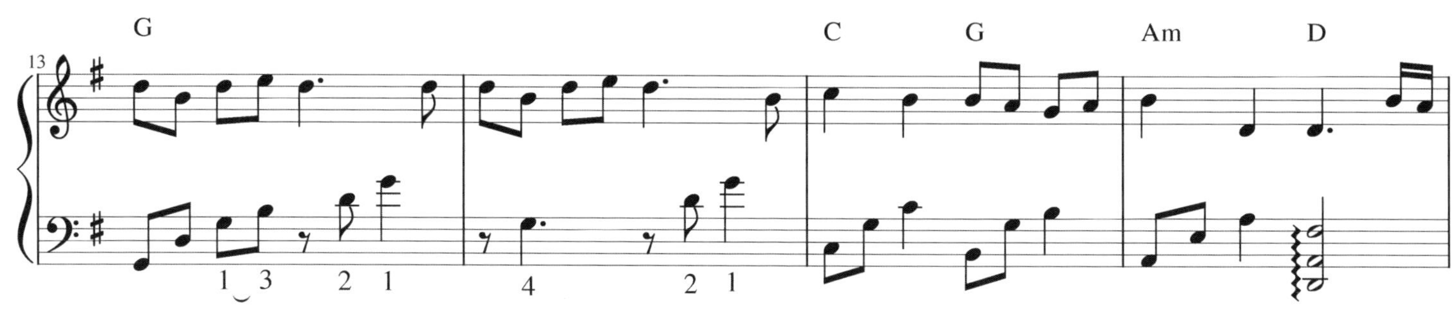

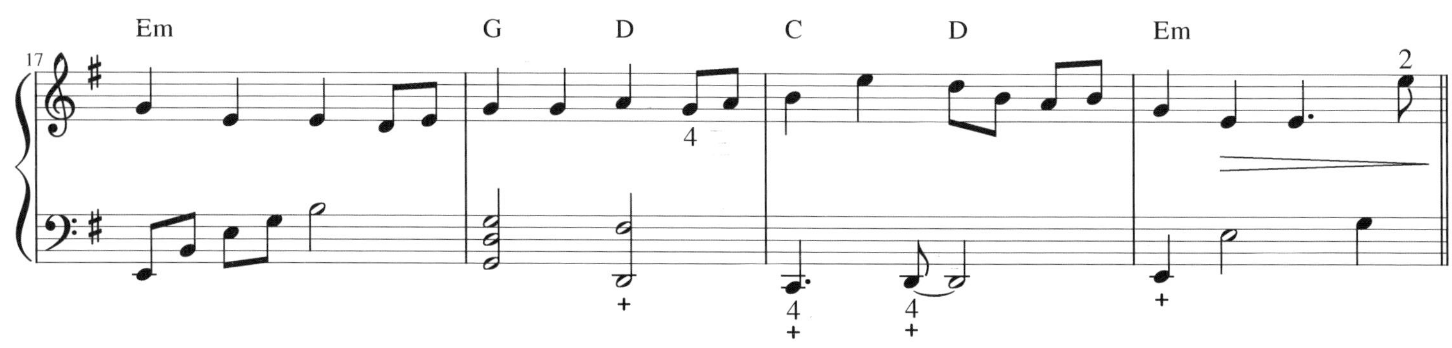

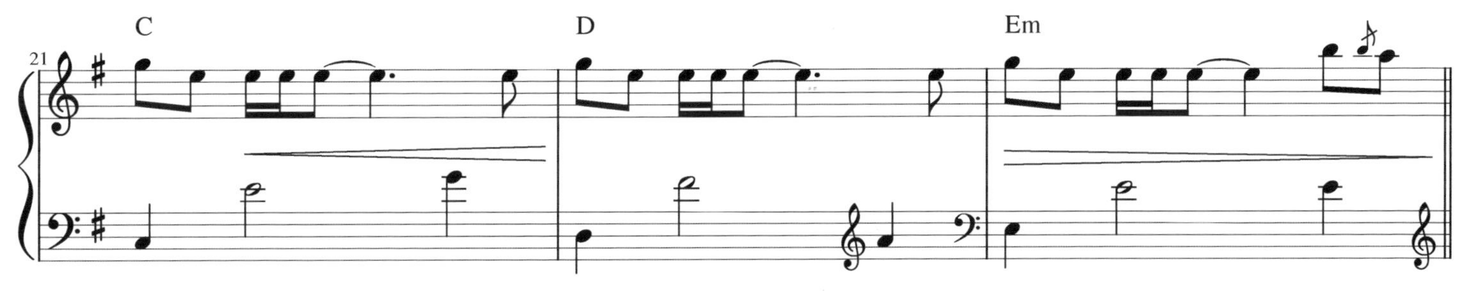
C
D
Em
21

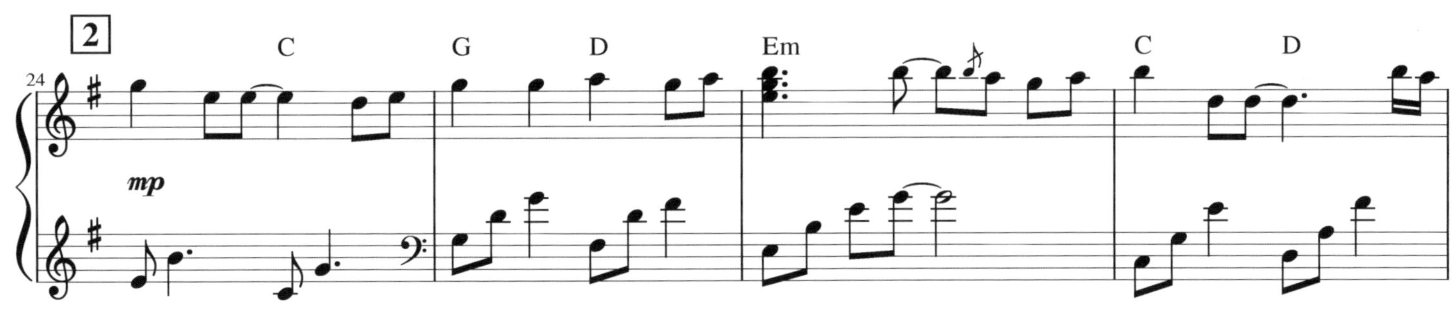
2
C
G
D
Em
C
D
24
mp

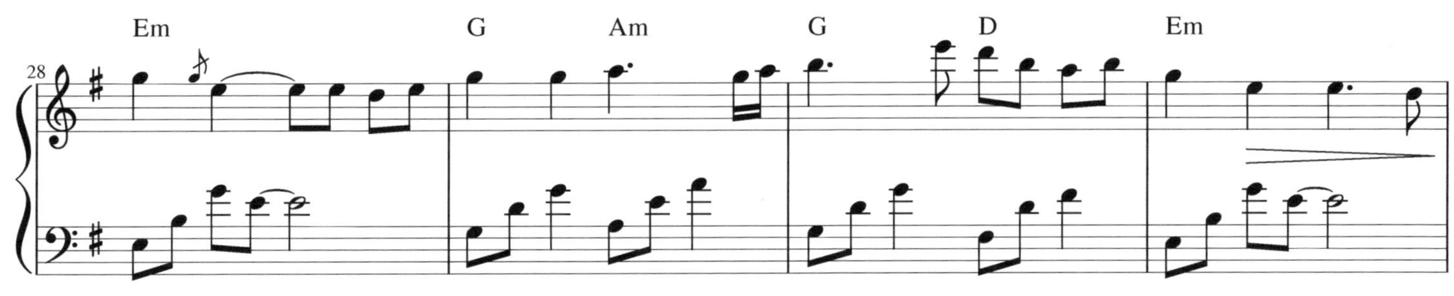
Em
G
Am
G
D
Em
28

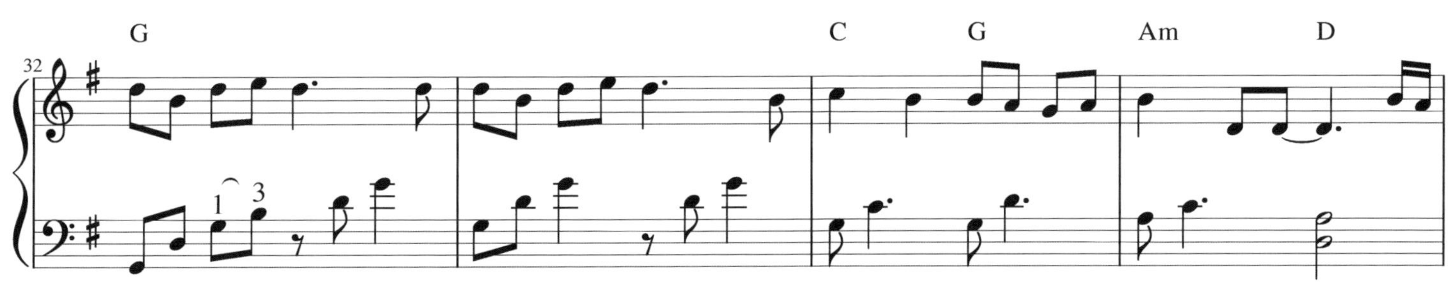
G
C
G
Am
D
32
1
3

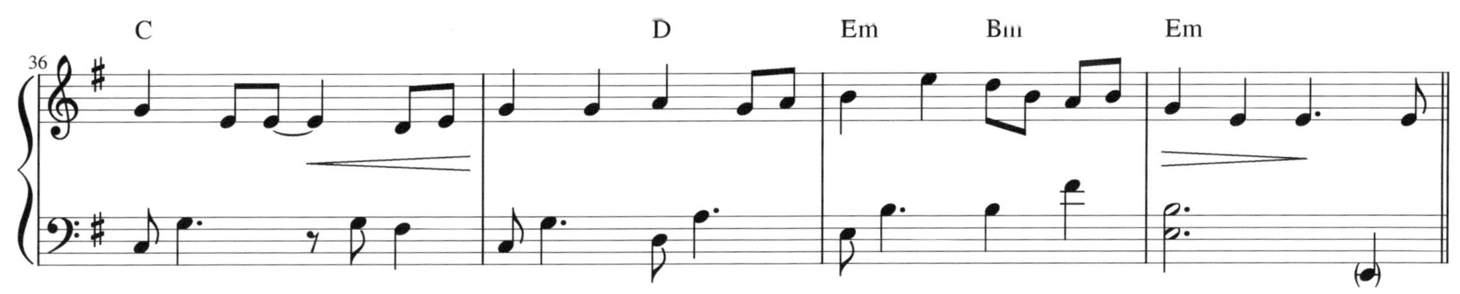
C
D
Em
Bm
Em
36

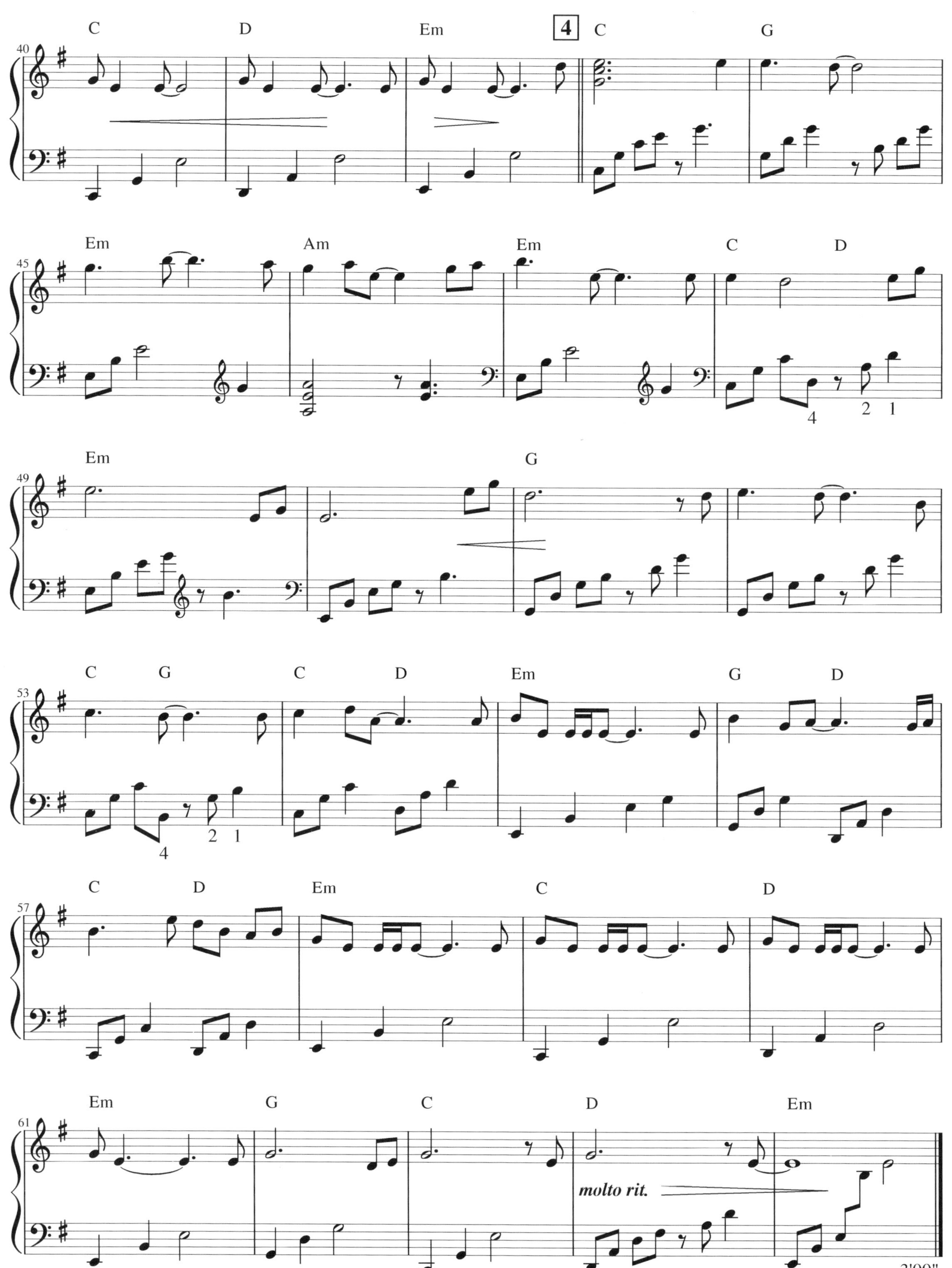
C D Em 4 C G
Em Am Em C D
Em G
C G C D Em G D
C D Em C D
Em G C D Em
molto rit.
3'00"

Ae Fond Kiss

Air, Traditional Scottish
Arranged by Stephanie Claussen

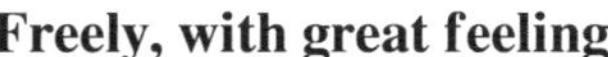

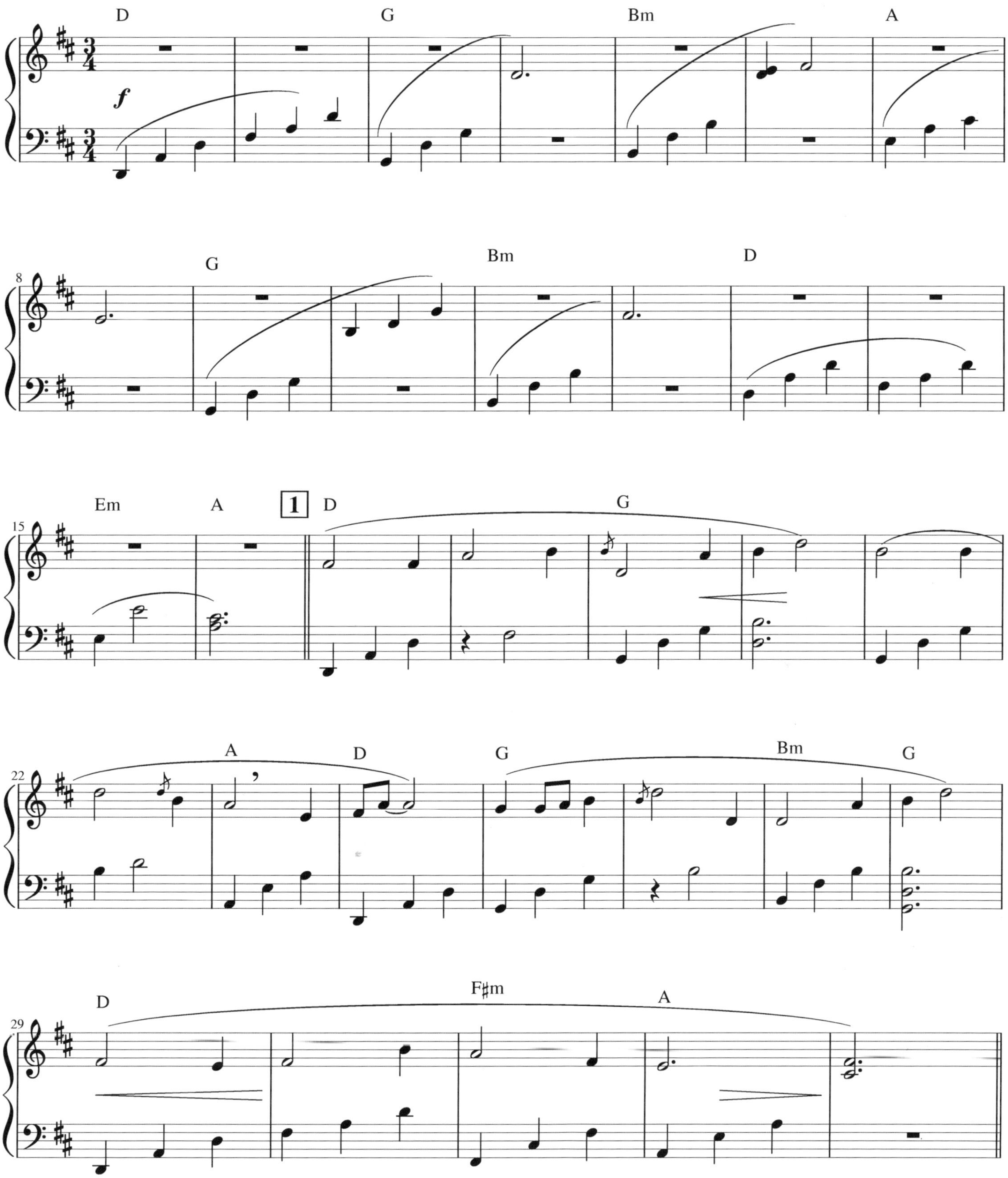

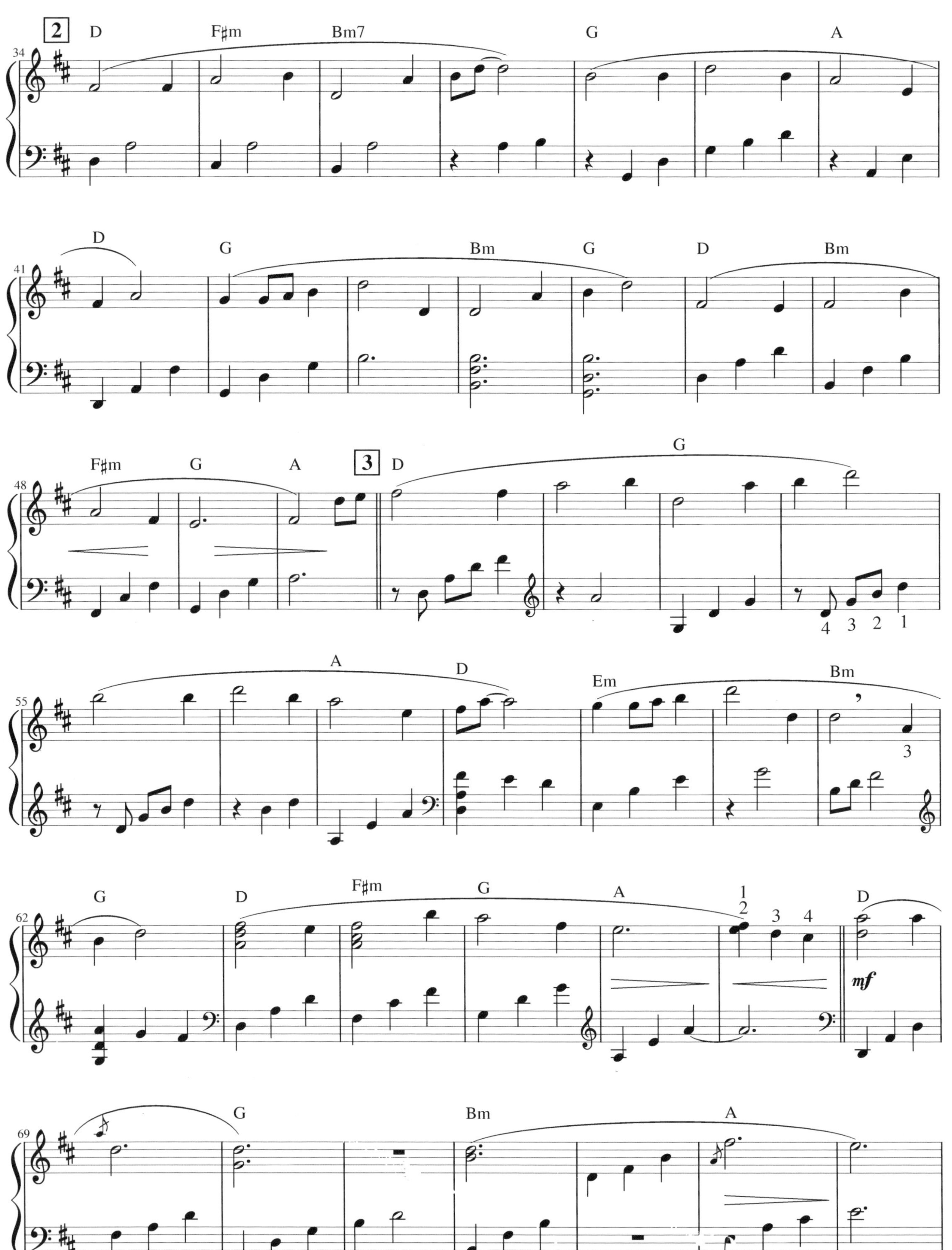
2
D
F♯m
Bm7
G
A
D
G
Bm
G
D
Bm
F♯m
G
A
3
D
G
A
D
Em
Bm
G
D
F♯m
G
A
D
mf
G
Bm
A

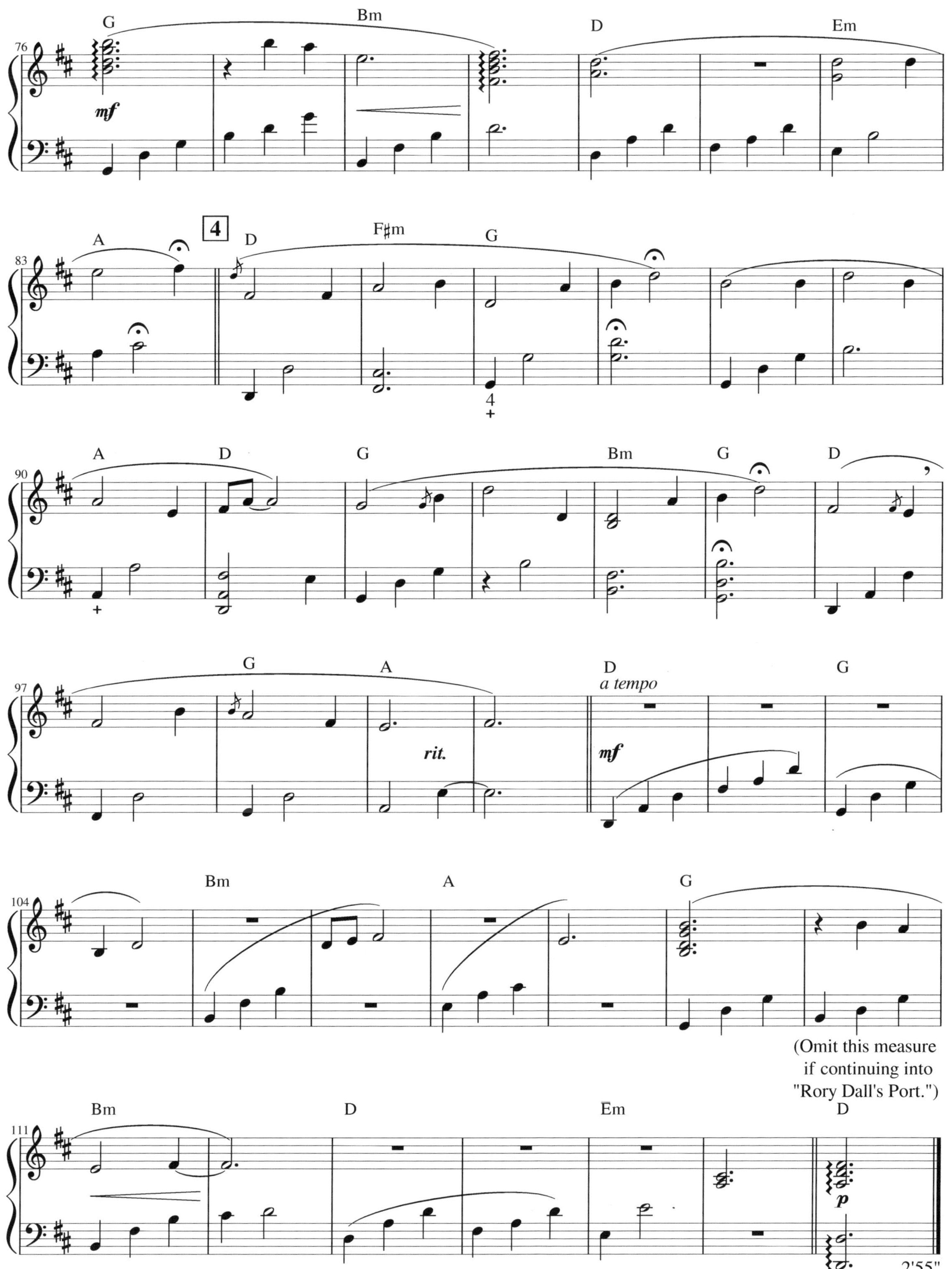
G
Bm
D
Em
mf
A
4
D
F♯m
G
A
D
G
Bm
G
D
G
A
D
a tempo
G
rit.
mf
Bm
A
G
(Omit this measure
if continuing into
"Rory Dall's Port.")
Bm
D
Em
D
p
2'55"

Rory Dall's Port

by Rory Dall
Arranged by Stephanie Claussen

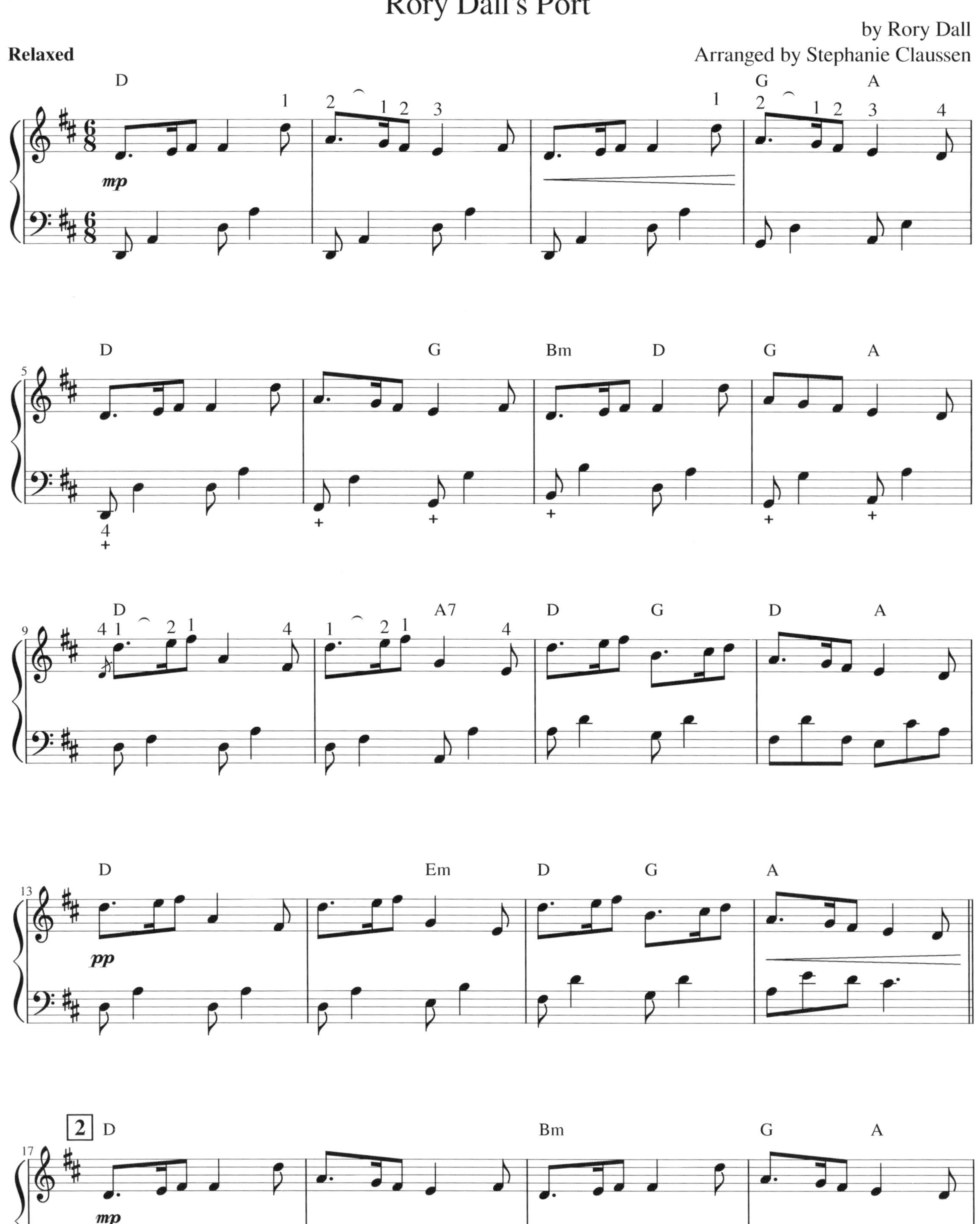

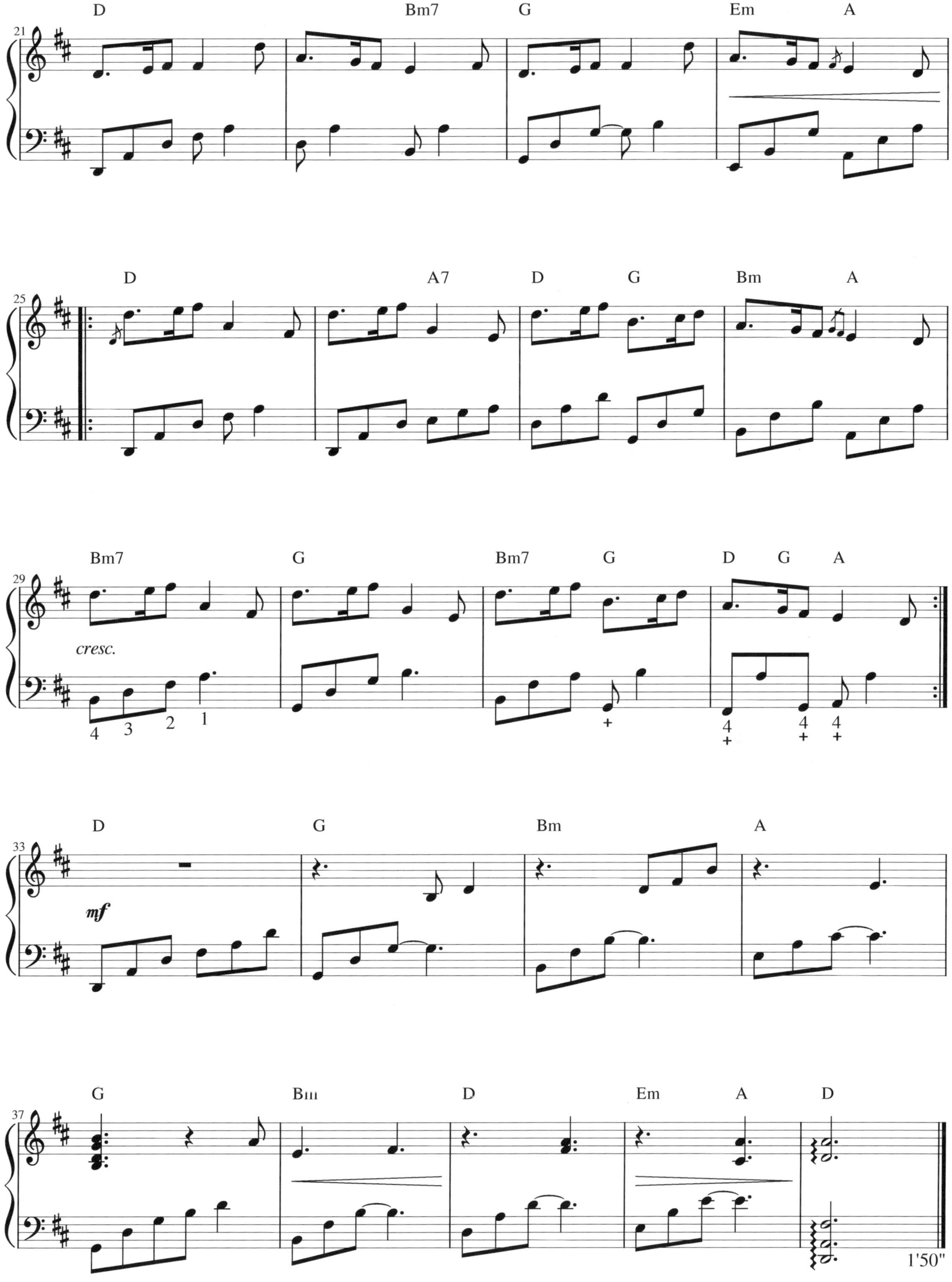

21 D Bm7 G Em A

25 D A7 D G Bm A

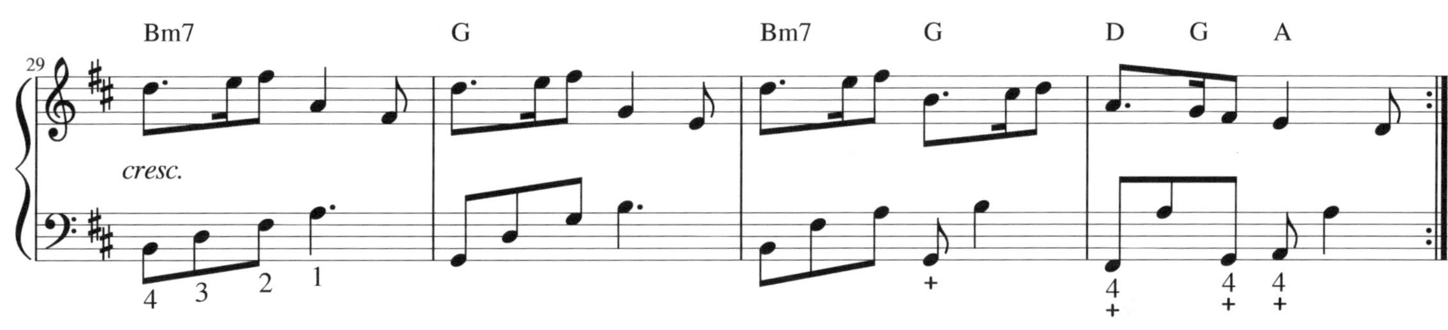

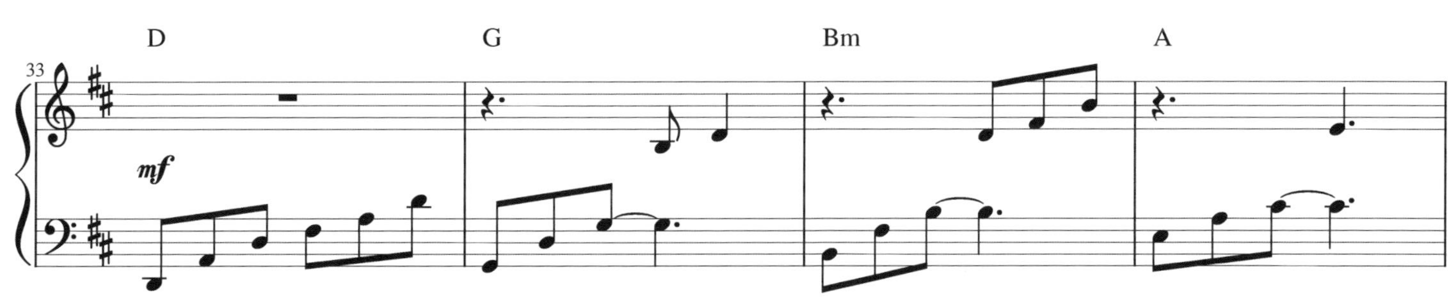

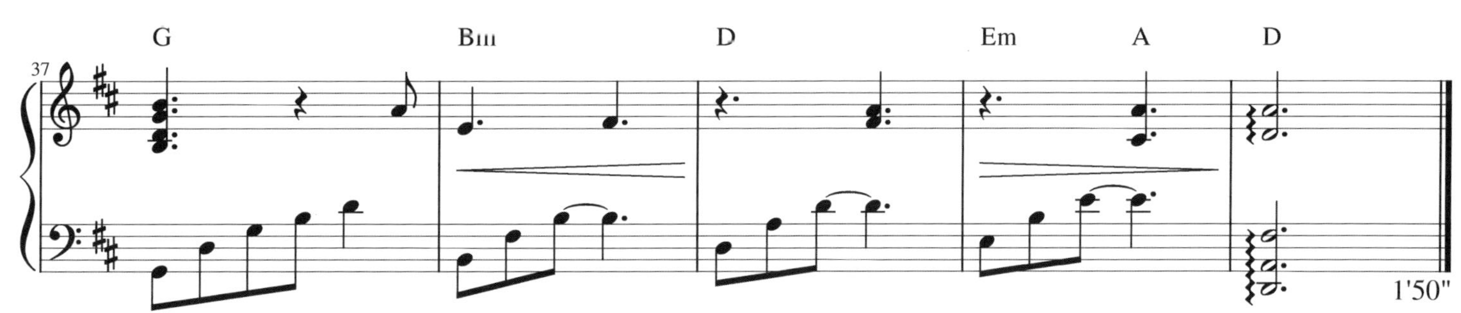

The Star of the County Down

Traditional Irish
Arranged by Stephanie Claussen

Waltz, with emphasis on beat 1

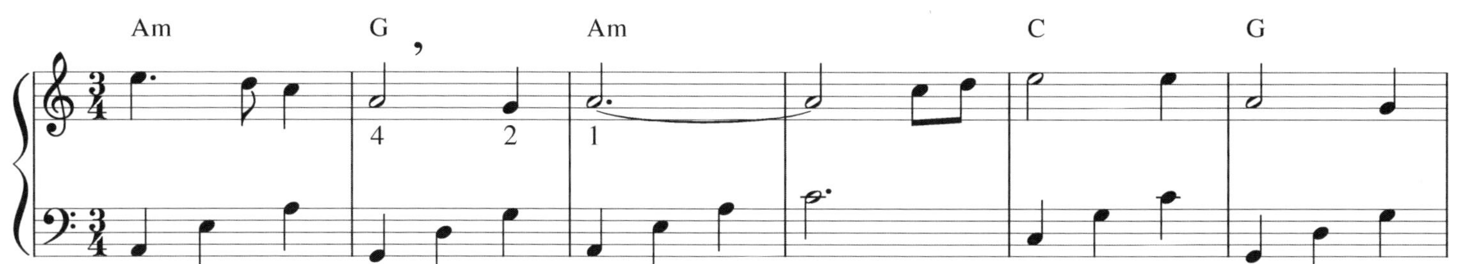

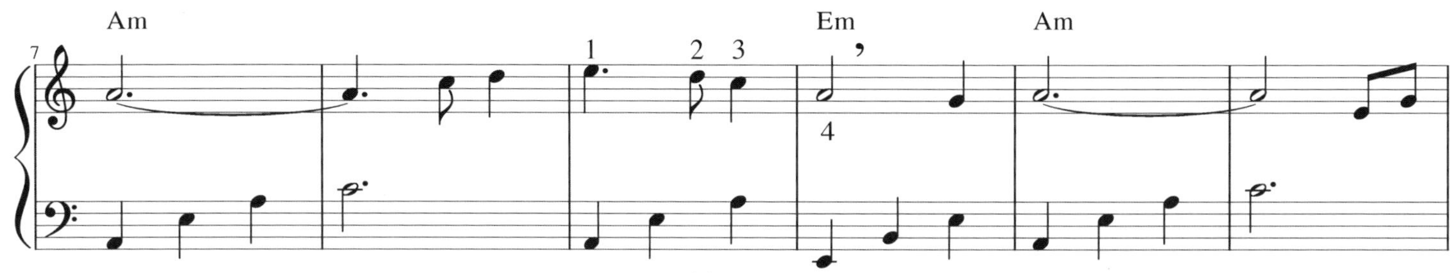

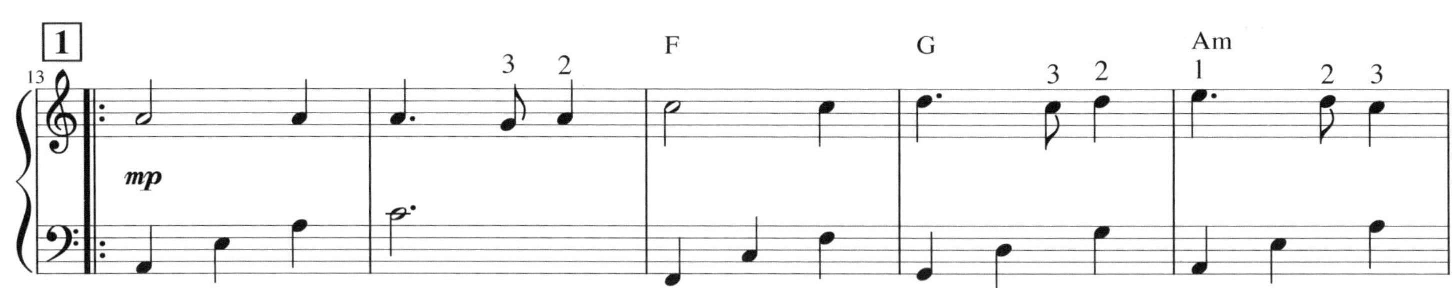

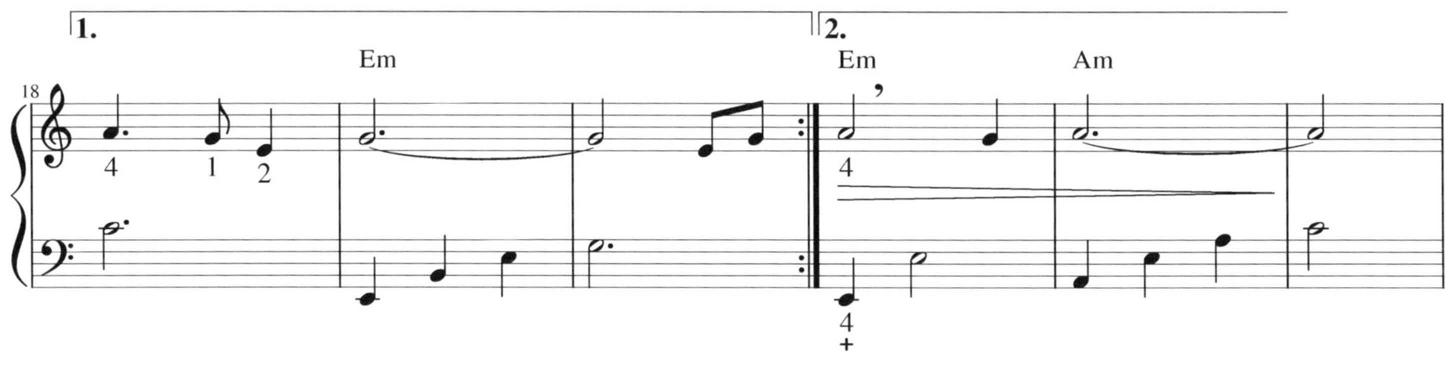

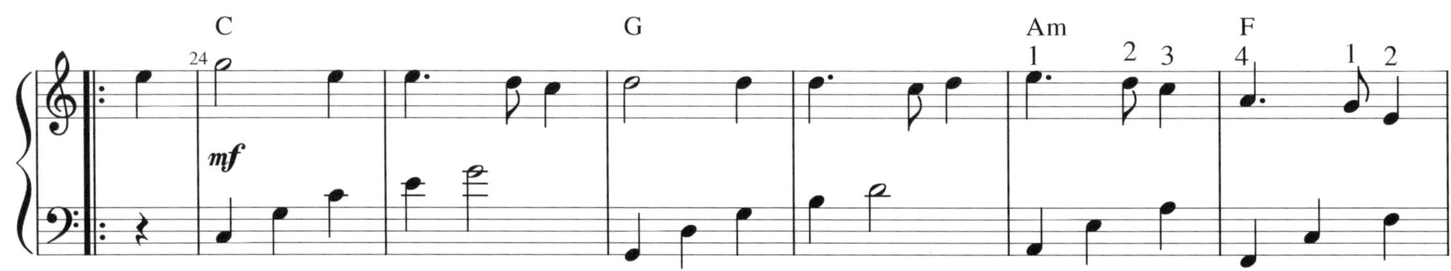

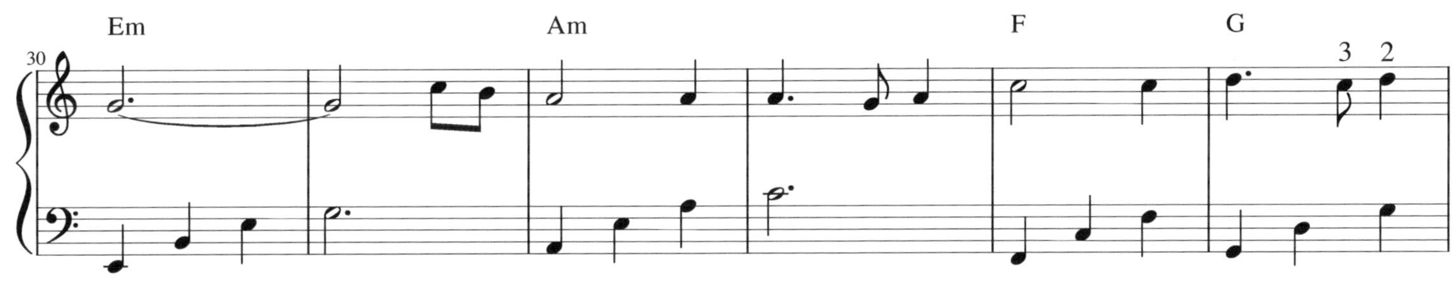
Em
Am
F
G
3 2
30

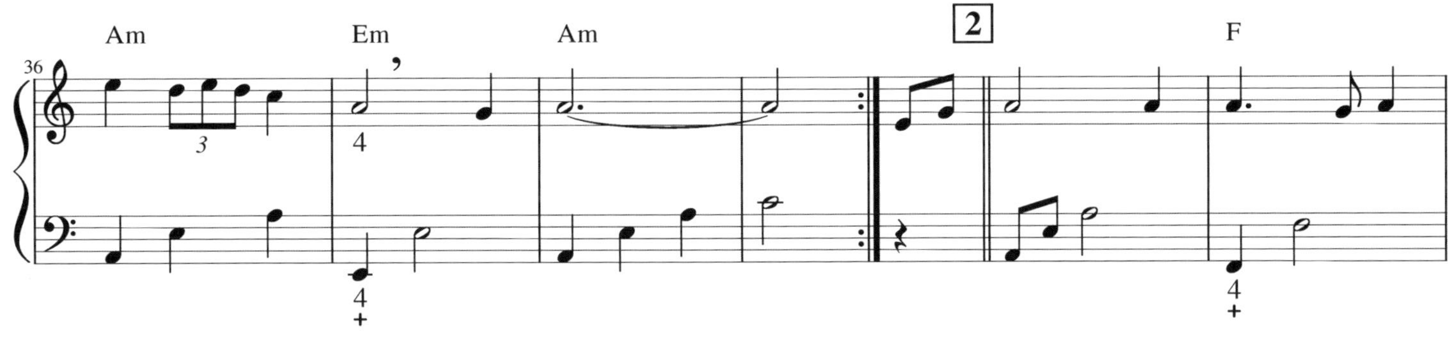
Am
Em
Am
2
F
36
3
4
4
+
4
+

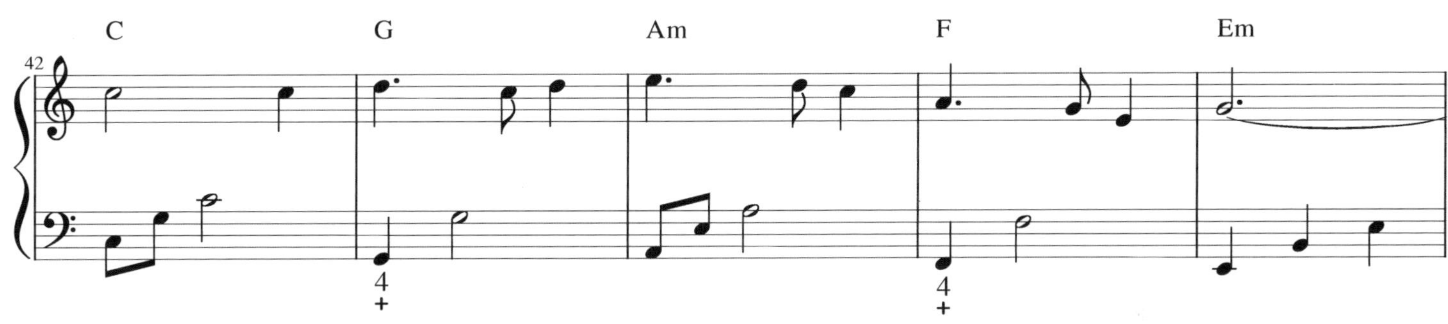
C
G
Am
F
Em
42
4
+
4
+

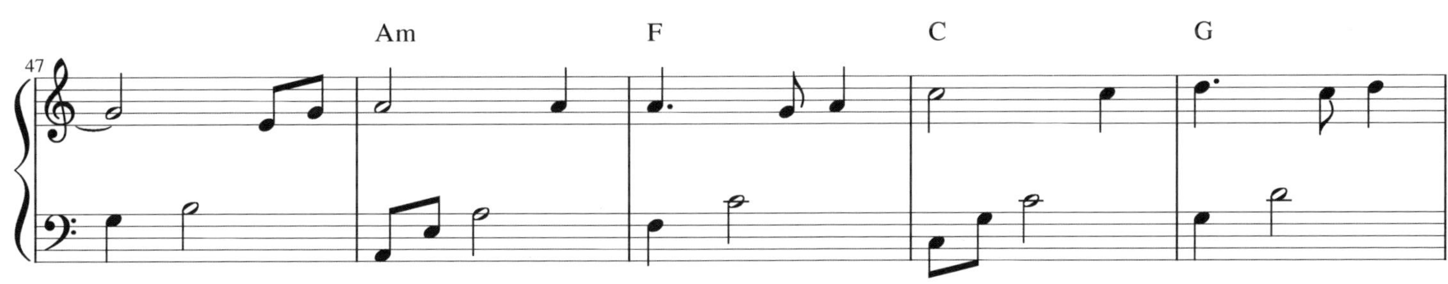
Am
F
C
G
47

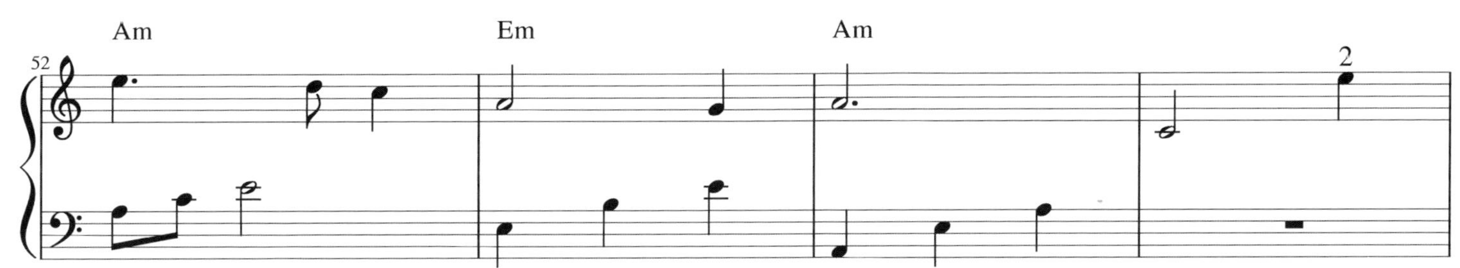
Am
Em
Am
2
52

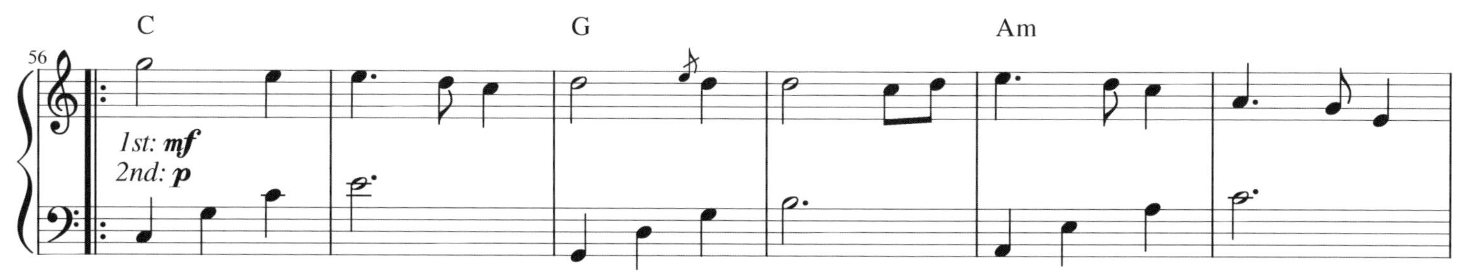

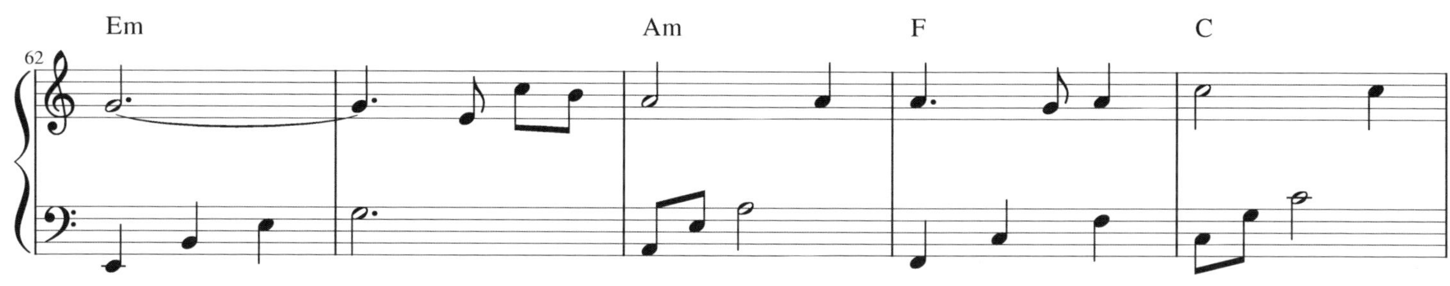

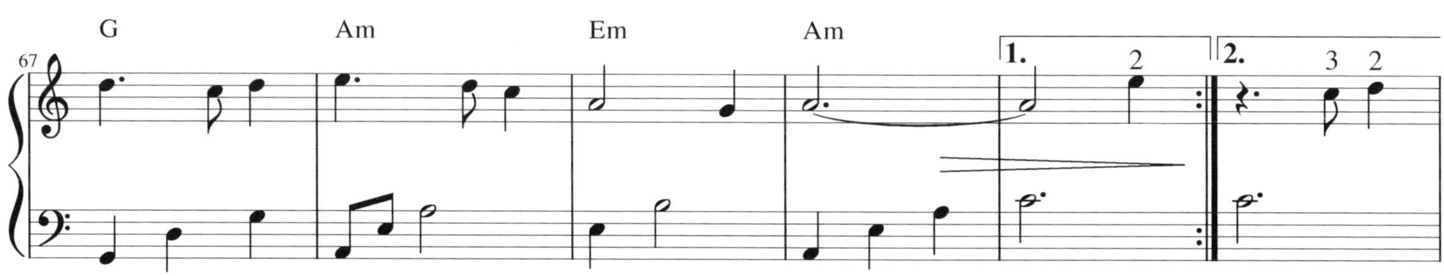

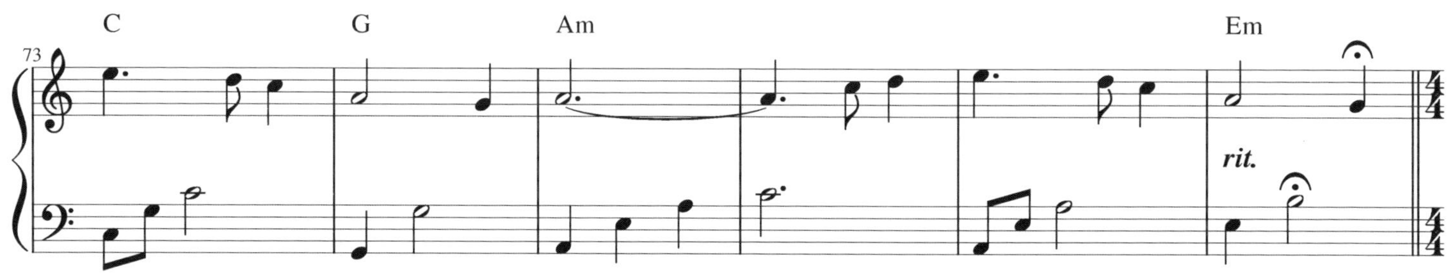

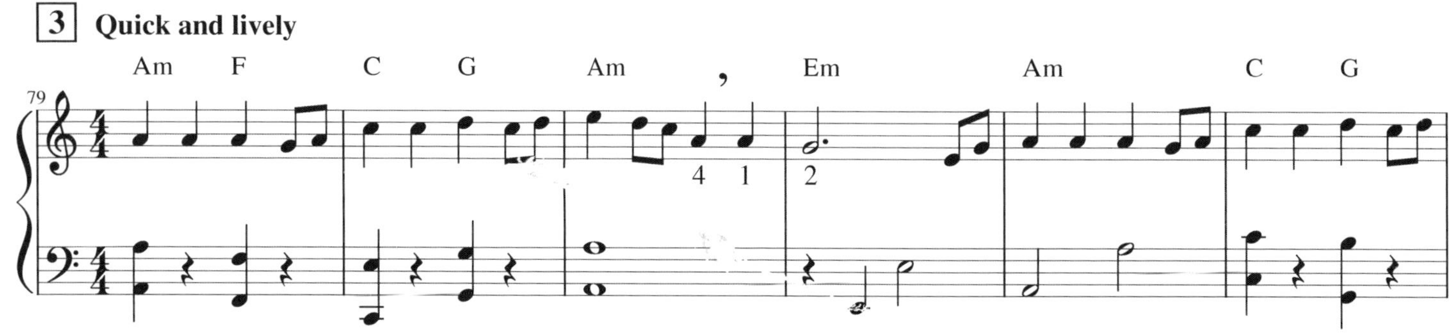

All left-hand octaves, broken or otherwise, should be played flat.

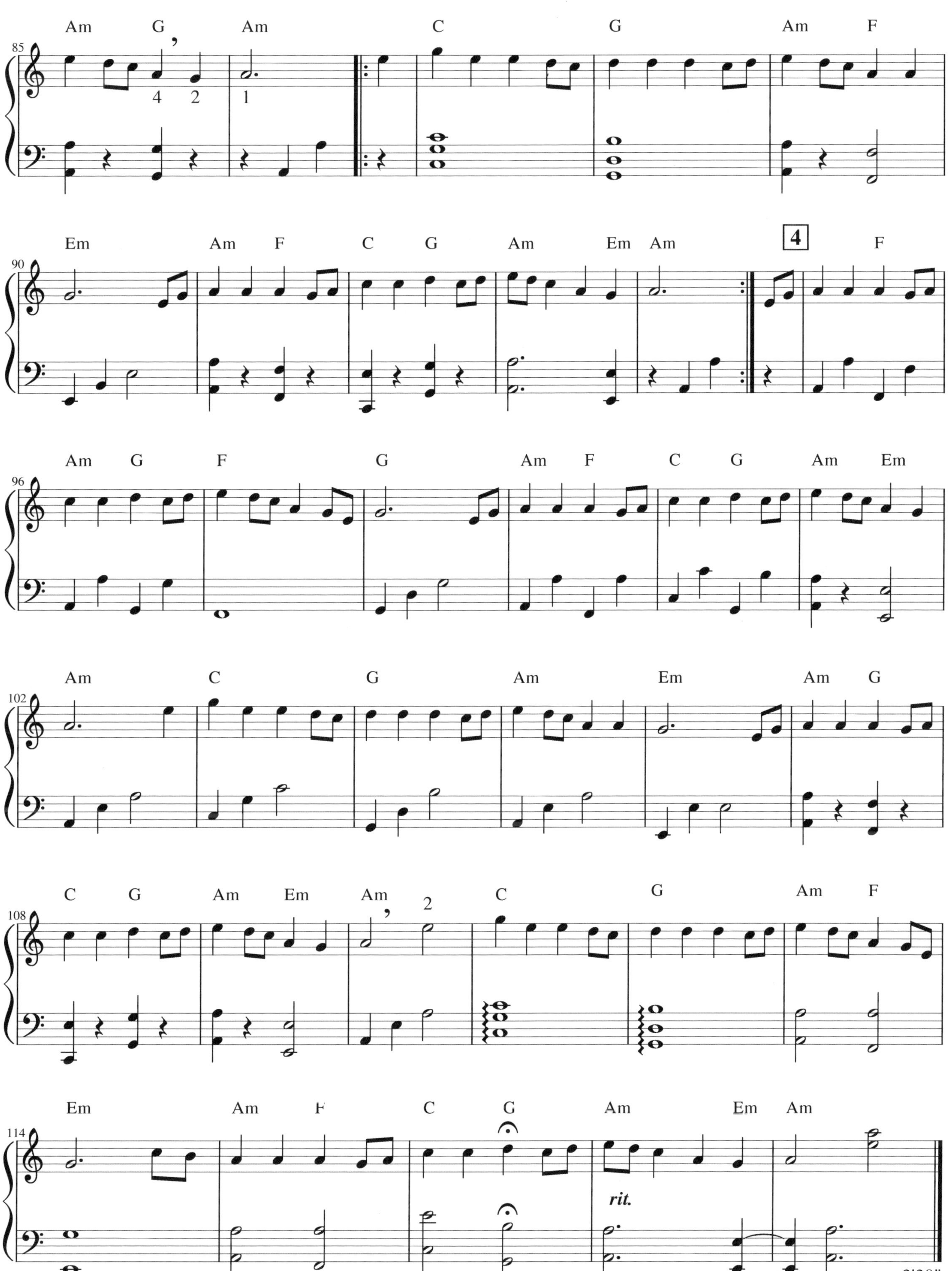

Am G Am C G Am F
85
4 2 1
Em Am F C G Am Em Am
4
F
90
Am G F G Am F C G Am Em
96
Am C G Am Em Am G
102
C G Am Em Am C G Am F
2
108
Em Am F C G Am Em Am
114
rit.
3'30"

About the Author

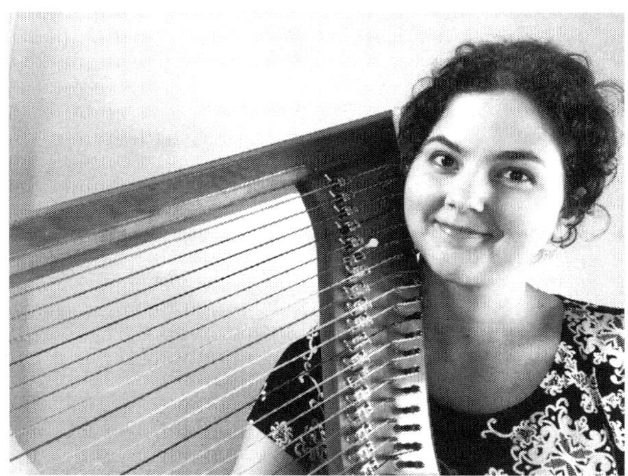

Minnesota-based harpist Stephanie Claussen is a performer, teacher and arranger. With interests that span the Celtic and classical harp worlds, she performs her own mixture of Scottish tunes, J.S. Bach, and anything that sounds medieval or French. In 2018 she won the title of US National Scottish Harp Champion, playing "The Duke of Fife's Welcome to Deeside," "Brose and Butter," and "Ca' the Yowes to the Knowes" among other tunes.

Claussen has released multiple solo albums as well as a book of harp arrangements entitled *Light so Brilliant: Christmas Carols and Tunes for Solo Harp*. When not making music, she enjoys repainting her walls and drinking English Breakfast tea out of a real teacup.

For information on performances and recordings by Stephanie Claussen, visit: www.StephanieClaussen.com. Purchase the album *The Road Home from Skye: Scottish and Irish Tunes* wherever music is sold.